SHEPHERD'S NOTES

When you need a guide through the Scriptures

D0017859

1,2 *Chronicles*

BROADMAN
&HOLMAN
PUBLISHERS

Nashville, Tennessee

Broadman & Holman Publishers
Nashville, Tennessee
All rights reserved
Printed in the United States of America

0–8054–9064–7
Dewey Decimal Classification: 221.60
Subject Heading: BIBLE. O.T. CHRONICLES
Library of Congress Card Catalog Number: 97–51488

Unless otherwise stated all Scripture citation is from the HOLY BIBLE, NEW INTER-
NATIONAL VERSION®. Copyright © 1973, 1978, 1984 by International Bible So-
ciety. Used by permission of Zondervan Publishing House. All Rights Reserved. The
"NIV" and "New International Version" trademarks are registered in the United States
Patent and Trademark Office by International Bible Society. Use of either trademark
requires the permission of International Bible Society. Scripture citations marked
NRSV are from the New Revised Standard Version of the Bible, copyright © 1989 by
the Division of Christian Education of the National Council of Churches of Christ in
the United States of America. Used by permission. All rights reserved. Scripture citations marked NASB are from the New American Standard Bible. ©The Lockman
Foundation, 1960, 1962, 1968, 1971, 1973, 1975, 1977. Used by permission.

Library of Congress Cataloging-in-Publication Data
I and II Chronicles / [edited by] Winfried Corduan.
    p. cm.   — (Shepherd's notes)
    Includes bibliographical references.
    ISBN 0–8054–9064–7 (pbk.)
    1. Bible. O.T. Chronicles—Study and teaching. I. Corduan, Winfried.
    II. Series
BS1345.5.A17   1998
221'.607—dc21

                                                          97–51488
                                                          CIP

1 2 3 4 5 6   03 02 01 00 99 98

SHEPHERD'S NOTES

CONTENTS

Foreword vi

How to Use This Book vii

Introduction 1

Genealogies (1 Chronicles 1–9) 5

King Saul (10:1–14) 18

The Reign of King David (11–29) 21

The Reign of Solomon
(2 Chronicles 1–9) 50

The Kings of Judah (2 Chron. 10–36) ..62

Reference Sources 93

FOREWORD

Dear Reader:

Shepherd's Notes are designed to give you a quick, step-by-step overview of every book of the Bible. They are not meant to be substitutes for the biblical text; rather, they are study guides intended to help you explore the wisdom of Scripture in personal or group study and to apply that wisdom successfully in your own life.

Shepherd's Notes guide you through the main themes of each book of the Bible and illuminate fascinating details through appropriate commentary and reference notes. Historical and cultural background information brings the Bible into sharper focus.

Six different icons, used throughout the series, call your attention to historical-cultural information, Old Testament and New Testament references, word pictures, unit summaries, and personal application for everyday life.

Whether you are a novice or a veteran at Bible study, I believe you will find *Shepherd's Notes* a resource that will take you to a new level in your mining and applying the riches of Scripture.

In Him,

David R. Shepherd
Editor-in-Chief

HOW TO USE THIS BOOK

DESIGNED FOR THE BUSY USER

Shepherd's Notes for 1 & 2 Chronicles is designed to provide an easy-to-use tool for getting a quick handle on these significant Bible books' important features, and for gaining an understanding of their messages. Information available in more difficult-to-use reference works has been incorporated into the *Shepherd's Notes* format. This brings you the benefits of many advanced and expensive works packed into one small volume.

Shepherd's Notes are for laymen, pastors, teachers, small-group leaders and participants, as well as the classroom student. Enrich your personal study or quiet time. Shorten your class or small-group preparation time as you gain valuable insights into the truths of God's Word that you can pass along to your students or group members.

DESIGNED FOR QUICK ACCESS

Bible students with time constraints will especially appreciate the timesaving features built into the *Shepherd's Notes*. All features are intended to aid a quick and concise encounter with the heart of the messages of 1 & 2 Chronicles.

Concise Commentary. 1 & 2 Chronicles provide a fresh interpretation of Israel's monarchy. Short sections provide quick "snapshots" of the narrative and themes of these books, highlighting important points.

Outlined Text. Summarizing outlines cover the entire texts of 1 & 2 Chronicles. This is a valuable feature for following each narrative's flow.

Shepherd's Notes. These summary statements or capsule thoughts appear at the close of every key section of the narratives. While functioning in part as a quick summary, they also deliver the essence of the message presented in the sections which they cover.

Icons. Various icons in the margin provide information that enhances the understanding of 1 & 2 Chronicles.

Sidebars and Charts. These specially selected features provide additional background information to your study or preparation. Charts offer a quick overview of important subjects. Sidebars include definitions as well as cultural, historical, and biblical insights

Maps. These are placed at appropriate places in the book to aid your understanding and study of a text or passage.

Questions to Guide Your Study. These thought-provoking questions and discussion starters are designed to encourage interaction with the truth and principles of God's Word.

DESIGNED TO WORK FOR YOU
Personal Study. Using the *Shepherd's Notes* with a passage of Scripture can enlighten your study and take it to a new level. At your fingertips is information that would require searching several volumes to find. In addition, many points of application occur throughout the volume, contributing to personal growth.

Teaching. Outlines frame the texts of 1 & 2 Chronicles, providing a logical presentation of their messages. Capsule thoughts designated as "Shepherd's Notes" provide summary statements for presenting the essence of key points and events. Application icons point out personal application of the messages of these books. Historical Context icons indicate where cultural and historical background information is supplied.

Group Study. Shepherd's Notes can be an excellent companion volume to use for gaining a quick but accurate understanding of the messages of 1 & 2 Chronicles. Each group member can benefit by having his or her own copy. The *Note's* format accommodates the study of themes throughout 1 & 2 Chronicles. Leaders may use its flexible features to prepare for group sessions or use them during group sessions. Questions to guide your study can spark discussion of 1 & 2 Chronicles's key points and truths to be discovered .

LIST OF MARGIN ICONS USED IN 1 & 2 CHRONICLES

Shepherd's Notes. Placed at the end of each section, a capsule statement provides the reader with the essence of the message of that section.

Old Testament Reference. Used when the writer refers to Old Testament passages or when Old Testament passages illuminate a text.

New Testament Reference. Used when the writer refers to New Testament passages that are related to or have a bearing on the passage's understanding or interpretation.

Historical Background. To indicate historical, cultural, geographical, or biographical information that sheds light on the understanding or interpretation of a passage.

Personal Application. Used when the text provides a personal or universal application of truth.

Word Picture. Indicates that the meaning of a specific word or phrase is illustrated so as to shed light on it.

In the English Bible, 1 and 2 Chronicles are the last two lengthy historical books of the Old Testament. A chronicle is a running account of historical events; in this case it is the account of events in the kingdom of Judah from the time of King David until the Babylonian Exile.

In the ancient Hebrew scrolls, Chronicles was called the "events or annals of the day," thus creating the idea of a "journal" or "diary" of Jewish history.

In terms of the time frame covered, the Chronicles run parallel to 2 Samuel and 1 and 2 Kings. But the Chronicles do not just repeat the other books. They address only some of the same events as the earlier books, and when they do, they often add a lot of new information. The rough layout of the two sets of books is this:

2 SAMUEL	1 CHRONICLES
Reign of King David:	Genealogies;
David's warfare, sins,	Reign and administration
and personal struggles	of King David

1 KINGS	2 CHRONICLES
Reign of Solomon and	Reign of Solomon
kings of Israel and	and kings of
Judah	Judah only

2 KINGS
Reign of kings of Israel and Judah

It would be a serious mistake, however, to think of 1 and 2 Chronicles only as filling in the gaps left by the other books, let alone as a mere

Ezra was a direct descendant of the high priests. He led a large group of Jews in the second return from the Exile in 458 B.C. (the first one having transpired in 536 B.C.). In Jerusalem, Ezra led a revival in which he called the people back to their heritage and the faithful service of God. We know from extrabiblical sources that Ezra's friend Nehemiah possessed a large library which would have been available to Ezra in reviewing Judah's history.

duplication. The author of Chronicles, to whom we shall refer as "the chronicler," had his own purpose. Under divine inspiration, he chose exactly the material that would bring his message home.

AUTHOR AND OCCASION

The Chronicles do not tell us who their author was, and nothing substantive hinges on being able to identify him. From information within the books, we can be quite certain that it was not written until some time after Judah returned from the Babylonian Exile (2 Chron. 36:22–23). Comparison with the book of Ezra shows a lot of similarity in style, content, and outlook. No wonder, then, that there is a long-standing tradition that Ezra the Scribe himself was the author of the Chronicles in the last part of the fifth century B.C.

An interesting feature of Chronicles is that the author used numerous different written sources and frequently refers his reader to them. They include some of our present biblical books such as 1 and 2 Kings, but also others such as "The Records of Shemaiah the Prophet."

PURPOSE AND POINT OF VIEW

There are several points of distinction for 1 and 2 Chronicles which together enable us to reconstruct what their purpose may have been:

1. Focus on the kingdom of Judah, particularly on its origin with King David;
2. Inclusion of a lot of lists, many of them genealogies;
3. Special attention paid to the priests, Levites, and the Temple.

If we try to think of a situation for which these points might be called for, we can put together the following setting for the writing of

Chronicles: It had already been a hundred years or so after the Jews were allowed to return from the Babylonian Exile, but they still had not recovered physically or spiritually from the ordeal. Specifically, in light of all the events, they were struggling with the notion that they were unique as God's chosen people. In response to this malaise, the author wrote Chronicles in order to clarify that:

1. Despite many difficulties, God has preserved the nation. They are still the same people as King David's mighty empire; and

2. God has provided His people a unique way of relating to Him through the priests and the Temple. The people are expected to be faithful to this relationship.

By reminding his readers of these two points, the chronicler encouraged them to pursue their lives as God's people with renewed vigor.

PREPARATION FOR STUDY

First and Second Chronicles are challenging to the modern reader in several respects:

1. The lengthy lists of names seem boring and unimportant. But the chronicler has scattered a lot of little nuggets within these lists, including details about characters that we know from other books of the Bible and brief stories that break the monotony.

2. Like other books of the Bible, Chronicles sometimes presents a very harsh picture of warfare as well as of sin and its consequences. This is surely not easy reading for anyone whose picture of God is mushy and sentimental. Instead, the books reveal a stern, unadorned image of life under the lordship of God. However,

Comparison of Chronicles with 1 and 2 Kings shows that from time to time there are discrepancies between numbers listed, e.g., in the sizes of armies. Liberal scholars have jumped to the conclusion that Chronicles deliberately exaggerates the numbers in order to create an impression of great glory. However, closer inspection shows that approximately half the time the numbers in Chronicles are lower than in Kings. Most of the differences are probably due to scribal error in copying the scrolls.

The gospel only makes sense in the light of sin and judgment. Apart from God's saving grace, we are all condemned by sin. Remember Christ's own disciples said: "This is a hard teaching. Who can accept it?" (John 6:60) and "Who can then be saved?" The answer lies in what God Himself has done.

this realistic picture highlights two important points: First, the consequences of sin are devastating, but second, God will bless and forgive those who come to Him, no matter how desperate the situation seems.

BASIC OUTLINE OF 1 AND 2 CHRONICLES

I. Genealogies (1 Chron. 1–9)
   A. Adam to the Twelve Tribes (1:1–2:2)
   B. The Twelve Tribes (2:3–9:44)
II. King Saul (1 Chron. 10)
III. King David (1 Chron. 11–29)
IV. King Solomon (2 Chron. 1–9)
V. Kings of Judah (2 Chron. 10–36)

QUESTIONS TO GUIDE YOUR STUDY

1. What are some specific points of distinction between the books of Samuel, Kings, and Chronicles?
2. How do the distinctives of Chronicles reveal its purpose?
3. What does it mean to today's readers to know that God has guided the history of His chosen people with a steadfast hand?

GENEALOGIES (1 CHRONICLES 1–9)

Genealogies play an important role in biblical history because they establish continuity in how God has related to His creatures. The New Testament begins where the genealogies in Chronicles leave off: Christ is the descendant of the kings of Judah (Matt. 1:1–17).

ADAM TO THE TWELVE TRIBES (1 CHRON. 1:1–2:2)

The first section of Chronicles is occupied with genealogies. It is important to recognize that often the links presented span more than one generation. In other words, someone mentioned as "son" is not necessarily the immediate biological son of the person ahead of him, but a descendant, perhaps his grandson, a great-grandson, or even someone further removed.

Chronicles follows a specific pattern in presenting most of the genealogies. As the chronicler proceeded, he gave us the less important branches of a line before going to the crucial one from which the line was continued.

■ *The genealogies show that there is continuity*
■ *in God's people through history.*

Adam to Noah (1:1–3)

First Chronicles opens at the very outset of history with Adam and his line of descendants through Seth. Cain's line is not mentioned here, and Abel presumably never had children before his untimely death. As the chronicler recited the names without introduction, fanfare, or explanation, the reader is immediately reassured: There is an unbroken thread in the lineage of God's people from the very outset.

The descendants of Japheth are identified with peoples of Asia Minor, Southeast Europe, and Southwest Asia. Ham's sons live in Northern Africa, Canaan, and Southwest Asia as well. From the Middle East across to Mesopotamia was the home for the early descendants of Shem.

Noah to Abraham (1:5–27)

The genealogy continues with Noah's three sons: Japheth, Ham, and Shem. Note how the names of some of the people became the names of their countries as well, e.g., Egypt and Canaan. The genealogy following Shem branches off at the point of Eber (the "Hebrew"). The reference to the division of the earth is most likely to the confusion at the tower of Babel (Gen. 11:9).

Abraham to Israel (1:28–34)

The listings continue according to the pattern of saving the most important branches for last. Thus, Abraham's descendants are enumerated beginning with Ishmael, Abraham's son from Hagar the maid. Next come the sons of Keturah, Abraham's second wife after the death of Sarah. Then Isaac is mentioned along with his sons, Esau and Israel or Jacob.

Isaac's Two Sons to the Twelve Tribes (1:35–2:2)

The Edomites were the descendants of Esau. He was called "Edom," "the Red," after he sold his birthright to Jacob for a dish of red food. The Edomites lived south of the Dead Sea in rugged mountainous territory. In the New Testament, they are referred to as the "Idumaeans."

Before identifiying Israel's descendants, Chronicles acknowledges Esau's offspring (vv. 35–37) and digresses even further. The descendants of Seir mentioned are an ancient people, probably predating the Edomites themselves. This passage concludes with a short list of Edomite chiefs (battle commanders). The Edomites were very important to the ensuing history of the people of Judah, as recounted in Chronicles. Finally, the chronicler states the names of the sons of Israel.

There is a clear thread of continuity running through human history beginning with Adam and leading to the twelve tribes which make up God's chosen people.

THE TWELVE TRIBES TO SAUL
(2:3–9:44)

Next follow lengthy listings pertaining to the twelve tribes. Judah, as the tribe of King David, receives quite a bit of attention. So does Levi, the tribe of priest and Temple attendants. The list culminates with Benjamin because the story continues with King Saul, who belongs to that tribe. A parenthetical listing of those who returned from Exile will precede the narrative of Saul's death. The chronicler does not always follow a clear sequence; several tribes pop up a few times.

Judah was the fourth son of Jacob. In spite of his several sins (Gen. 38), he became the leader among the twelve brothers. The tribe of Judah was the most populous; it received the first allocation in the Promised Land, a large territory to the south.

■ *The ancient people of God found their iden-*
■ *tity in their tribes, which played important*
■ *roles in the heritage of the nation.*

Judah to David (2:3–17)

The chronicler manages to pack a lot of scandal into the list to which David is connected. He mentions quite a few instances in which David's ancestors married outside the pure lineage. There are Judah's five sons, three from a Canaanite wife and two from his Canaanite daughter-in-law, Tamar. Of these latter two, Zerah became the ancestor of the notorious Achar (Achan), who caused trouble at the conquest of Canaan (Josh. 7), while Perez's line eventually picks up Ruth, the Moabitess. Also, David's own sister Abigail married an Ishmaelite. David was the descendant of Judah by way of Perez, Hezron, Ram, Boaz, and Jesse, among others.

■ *David was the descendant of Judah; this genea-*
■ *ology is a sometimes troubled line of descent.*

Further Lines within Judah (2:18–55)

This same Hezron, ancestor of David, is the axis around whom the rest of the chapter revolves. His son Ram continued the line to David. His other two sons, Caleb and Jerahmeel, are also prominent. The Caleb mentioned here is not the same person as the spy who trusted the Lord in the conquest (Num. 13:30).

In looking at these genealogies, it becomes obvious that, for the most part, the links representing the time in Egypt are shortened or omitted.

The Royal Line (3:1–24)

The chronicler now returns to David and provides a synopsis of his descendants. First, he mentions the six sons of David stemming from David's time as king in Hebron. We see some familiar and tragic names here: Amnon, the firstborn, who raped his sister Tamar (2 Sam. 13); Absalom, who rebelled against David (2 Sam. 15); and Adonijah, who tried against God's will to claim the throne during David's last days (1 Kings 1). Chronicles does not mention any of these incidents, but it goes on with a list of thirteen sons stemming from David's thirty-three years in Jerusalem. Of these, four are sons of Bathsheba (again, the episode of adultery is ignored), and among these, Solomon is listed last because David's royal line continues with him.

The subsequent list is a quick register of the kings of Judah. This roster continues through the Exile. We catch the name of Zerubbabel, the

Simeon was the second son of Jacob. The territory of Simeon was located to the south and west of Judah. But for reasons which are unclear, this tribe is reckoned with the northern tribes and the northern kingdom of Israel. This tribe had a hard life. Much of its territory was marginal desert land; both Judah and the Philistines expropriated some of its better stretches. Simeon essentially disappeared in the later Old Testament record.

governor of Judea after the return from the Exile. The line goes on a few more generations and ends a short while before the time of Ezra.

- ◼ *The kings of Judah represent an unbroken*
- ◼ *line going back to David.*

Further Genealogies within Judah (4:1–22)

Not all of the people in this passage are clearly related to each other. The chronicler partially filled in gaps from the listing in chapter 2 and partially provided further information of direct interest in its own right. Some of the important names mentioned include Othniel, the first judge (Judg. 3:7–11); Caleb, the spy (Num. 13), who was related to Othniel.

The Tribe of Simeon (4:24–43)

Simeon is the first of the so-called "northern" tribes inventoried. In order to survive, the Simeonites needed to expand their territory. Our passage mentions two occasions: first, when they claimed a piece of land which had once belonged to Hamites (Canaanites), and then again when they undertook an expedition against Edom. At this later time, the Simeonites finally eliminated the Amalekites for good, a task that had originally been given to King Saul, but which he did not carry out (1 Sam. 15).

The Tribe of Reuben (5:1–10)

The listing of names pertaining to Reuben verges on the perfunctory, probably because by the time of the writing of Chronicles the tribe had vanished. The tribe was among the first to be carried into Exile by the Assyrians.

Reuben was the firstborn of Jacob's sons. However, he had had intercourse with Bilhah, who was Jacob's concubine and his stepmother. Consequently, Reuben was deprived of his privileges as firstborn son; these privileges were given to Joseph instead. And, thus, the tribe would never achieve preeminence. Judah became the strongest tribe while the actual birthright belonged to the tribes descended from Joseph (Ephraim and Manasseh).

Like the tribe of Simeon, Reuben's tribe led an insignificant existence for most of the history of Israel.

Gad was Jacob's seventh son. The descendants of Gad lived on the east side of the Jordan River, just a little north of the Reubenites.

Manasseh was the younger son of Joseph, Jacob's eleventh son. There was no tribe of Joseph. Instead, Joseph's two sons, Ephraim and Manasseh, were each reckoned as the progenitors of their own tribes. Ephraim turned out to be the dominant tribe of the Northern Kingdom, and Manasseh also was extremely powerful and populous. Manasseh was so large, in fact, that this tribe received extensive land allocations on both sides of the Jordan River.

The Tribe of Gad (5:11–17)

Once again the chronicler provides us with very scant information. He credits what he knows to records which were kept at two different times: during the reigns of Jotham of Judah (751–736 B.C.) and of Jeroboam II of Israel (793–751 B.C.).

The Fate of the Eastern Tribes (5:18–24)

Even though Chronicles does not give us much genealogical information on Manasseh until the seventh chapter, the eastern half of this tribe is already included in this list along with its neighbors, Reuben and Gad, in order to make an important point. First, we learn of a war which the combined tribes of Reuben, Gad, and East Manasseh won against a number of Arabian tribes, led by the Hagrites, the descendants of Hagar, the mother of Ishmael.

The chronicler specified that this victory was due to the fact that the people trusted God. Then he noted a second, vastly different outcome after he gave us some brief notes on the half-tribe. He reported that the people stopped worshiping God and started to commit idolatry. As a result, we read that God Himself stirred up the Assyrian king Pul (who bore the royal name Tiglath Pileser) to carry these tribes into captivity. This divine judgment occurred before the rest of the northern tribes were conquered and deported.

■ *The tribes of Simeon, Reuben, Gad, and East*
■ *Manasseh carried their share of the heritage*
■ *of God's people. However, they vanished ear-*
■ *lier than some of the other tribes. For the lat-*
■ *ter three, disobedience was the reason.*

The Tribe of Levi (6:1–81)

The pointed interest of Chronicles in the priesthood becomes apparent in this chapter, with its lengthy inventory of Levitical families. Everyone presumably had some concern over their tribal identity, but for a Levite it was a matter of urgent necessity. This tribe received no large territory of its own, for Levi was the tribe of priests and Temple assistants. The priestly tribe was given special living areas throughout the land. Only people whose ancestry was beyond dispute were eligible for inclusion in this tribe's duties and benefits.

Levi was Jacob's third son. Together with Simeon, he was guilty of some barbaric behavior (Gen. 34; 49:5–7). Nevertheless, he was destined to be the forefather of the tribe of priests.

The Line of High Priests (vv. 1–15)

Of the genealogical information presented, the most important lineage goes from Levi to Aaron by way of Kohath and Amram. Here is clearly a case in which the chronicler skipped many generations, for the time from Levi to Aaron actually spanned roughly four hundred years. Now follows a list of high priests which is not intended to be complete either; later, Chronicles mentions a number of high priests who are left out here. The emphasis is on the continuity of the line within the priestly family. This initial record broke off with the Babylonian Exile when the first Temple was destroyed.

Levitical Clans (vv. 16–29)

Now the chronicler began to fill in the earlier register. He mentioned different clans who were derived from the sons of Levi. This list can appear extremely confusing because there are apparently no less than four men with the name of Elkanah. The last of them is the father of Samuel (1 Sam. 1).

Twelve psalms (50, 73–83) are ascribed to Asaph. This could refer to the fact that he composed them, that he performed them, or that they were a part of his family's heritage. In fact, we see in the Psalms that David dedicated many of his songs to the "head musician," which would, for a time at least, have been Asaph.

The Head Musicians (vv. 31–47)

Suddenly, we focus more directly on David's time. Although David did not build the Temple, as we read later, he rectified some of the disorder that had overtaken the worship practices of Israel in the later years of Samuel and during the time of Saul. David, the harpist and songwriter, installed three professional musicians as permanent ministers at the tabernacle. The chronicler gives us the detailed genealogies for these men, each of whom was descended from one of the three sons of Levi: Heman from Kohath, Asaph from Gershon, and Ethan from Merari.

The Priestly Line Again (vv. 49–53)

Once more this chapter reiterates the line of descent from Aaron, emphasizing that only those in this line were permitted to perform the sacrifices.

Town Allocations for Levi (vv. 54–81)

The tribe of Levi did not receive a large territory all its own, but the people had to live somewhere. Thus, Levi received towns scattered throughout the Promised Land at the time of the Conquest. The passage first mentions the descendants of Aaron, who were provided living space in Judah and Benjamin. The other Levite clans were placed in regions belonging to various tribes. After a general survey, the chronicler gives us more detailed information concerning the specific Levite families.

■ *Levi was responsible for the priestly sacri-*
■ *fices and Temple support. A member of this*
■ *tribe enjoyed certain special privileges; it*
■ *was important to know to which line within*
■ *the tribe one belonged.*

The Tribe of Issachar (7:1–5)

In this chapter, we receive brief notices concerning seven tribes, beginning with Issachar. We learn the names of Issachar's four sons (Tola, Puah, Jashub, and Shimron) and the fact that this tribe gave rise to a sizeable army. The number of 87,000 warriors for Issachar compares with 44,760 total for the combined army of the eastern tribes (5:18), 59,434 for Benjamin (counting all three clans in 7:7, 9, 11), and 26,000 for Asher (7:40).

Issachar was Jacob's seventh son. His tribe settled in the Promised Land just south of the Sea of Galilee.

The Tribe of Benjamin (7:6–12)

The chronicler gives us some preliminary information on Benjamin, specifically the names of his three sons (Bela, Becher, and Jediael) and the clans whom they generated. He reserves the rest of the information for a little later when the detailed genealogy of Benjamin will lead up to its favorite son, King Saul.

The Tribe of Naphtali (7:13)

The tribe of Naphtali receives a scant notice of only one verse. We learn only of Naphtali's four sons (Jahziel, Guni, Jezer, and Shillem)—nothing more.

The Tribe of Manasseh Again (7:14–19)

This section spells out a little more information concerning the half-tribe of Manasseh, this time probably focusing on the part of the tribe west

Benjamin was Jacob's twelfth son. His mother, Rachel, died in childbirth. The tribe of Benjamin lived north of Judah and south of Ephraim. At one point, the entire tribe was almost eliminated by the other tribes. Even though the tribe produced King Saul and his family—the rivals to David—when the kingdom eventually split, Benjamin sided with Judah.

Naphtali was Jacob's sixth son. When the tribes settled in the Promised Land, Naphtali's lot was drawn last. They settled in the area which we know from the New Testament as Galilee.

Ephraim was the younger son of Joseph. When Jacob blessed the two sons of Joseph, he deliberately put Ephraim ahead of his older brother, Manasseh (Gen. 48:19). As it turns out, Ephraim did become the more dominant. Frequently, the Old Testament refers to Ephraim as "Joseph"; the governance of the Northern Kingdom took place for the most part out of this tribe.

of the Jordan River. Manasseh's direct descendants became leaders of important clans.

The Tribe of Ephraim (7:20–29)

The information in this section incorporates a number of historical sidelights which paint a picture of the descendants of Ephraim as active and enterprising people.

The Tribe of Asher (7:30–40)

The genealogies of Asher given in this passage are straightforward and complimentary.

- *The chronicler provided information on the*
- *northern tribes as it was available to him.*
- *Some of the tribes took on different personal-*
- *ities, an insight reflected in the genealogies.*

Further Information on Benjamin (8:1–32)

In preparation for his discussion on King Saul, the chronicler now returned to the tribe of Benjamin. Some of the connections mentioned here are unclear. Apparently, the Ehud referred to here is Ehud son of Gera, of the tribe of Benjamin, who is described in the book of Judges (3:15) as the left-handed judge. We have no further information on the deportation alluded to in this connection.

The Descendants of Saul (8:33–40)

The immediate line of Saul begins with Jeiel, who had a son named Ner. Ner's son was named after his brother, Kish, and he became the father of Saul. The chronicler does not mention any of the early history of Saul. Eventually he will begin with Saul's last battle (chap. 10). In this context, he carries on the genealogy without any commentary and mentions Saul's sons. The best known of Saul's sons was Jonathan, David's close friend. There are enough links given here to carry us at least to the time of the Exile.

- *Even though the kingdom eventually*
- *belonged to David's descendants and not*
- *Saul's, it was still important to understand*
- *the links leading up to Saul and after him.*

Return from the Exile (9:1–9)

The chronicler has now concluded his inventory of the tribes of Israel.

Now we skip ahead to the time of the return from the Exile for a listing of some of the people who came back from the Babylonian captivity. We learn that the focal point of the return was Jerusalem, and that among the first to come back were people who were tied to the Temple service, e.g., priests and Levites. This is only natural since the edict to return to Judah was coupled with the command to rebuild the Temple (2 Chron. 36:23). Note in verse 3 that the tribes represented were Judah, Benjamin, Ephraim, and Manasseh, the latter two of which were of the Northern Kingdom. But when the listing becomes more specific, only Judah—with 690 heads of families—and Benjamin—with 956 heads of families—are enumerated.

Priests (9:10–13)

There were more priests (1,760) as heads of families than the number of lay families from Judah and Benjamin put together. Azariah is referred to as being "in charge of the house of God"; this venerable figure had already been high priest before the Exile (6:13). Surely he

Asher was the eighth son of Jacob. This tribe settled on the Mediterranean coast just south of the Phoenician territory. In spite of its relative insignificance, one of the descendants of this tribe—the prophetess Anna—perceived that the infant Jesus was the Savior.

Esh-Baal is the same as Ishbosheth, who was David's rival for the throne upon Saul's death (2 Sam. 1). Jonathan's son, Merib-Baal should be identified with Mephibosheth, to whom David showed kindness later in his reign (2 Sam. 9). Apparently, Merib-Baal was the only surviving member of Saul's clan, but we see that the lineage continued through him.

Dan and Zebulun (Jacob's fifth and tenth sons) are left out of the genealogies altogether. This omission may mean that the chronicler had no information, but it may also be that Dan in particular was odious to him. We should not be surprised that a chronicler in fifth century B.C. Judea had little sympathy for Dan. This tribe had originally been allocated a scanty area on the Mediterranean coast. Because this territory was too small, the Danites migrated to a location at the very north of the Promised Land. When the Northern Kingdom (Israel) broke off from the Kingdom of Judah, Dan became a center of idol worship in deliberate competition with the Temple in Jerusalem (1 Kings 12:29). From the vantage point of Chronicles' original readers who were supposed to renew their identity as God's people, Dan had little to offer.

would have been among those who wept when the rebuilt Temple was dedicated (Ezra 3:12).

Levites (9:14–16)

A quick overview of the main Levitical families who returned must suffice the reader at this point. We see that the clans of Asaph and Jeduthun, David's chief musicians, were both represented.

Gatekeepers (9:17–33)

According to verse 22, the office of gatekeeper of the sanctuary went back as far as the time of Samuel and was reinstituted by David. During David's lifetime, they officiated at the tent which served as sanctuary; after the Temple was built, they were attached to the permanent buildings. These men were security officials for the sanctuary; Samuel had seen for himself how abuse of the worship practices would lead to disastrous judgment (1 Sam. 2). The guards would live on the sacred grounds, close and open the gates, keep track of the utensils used by the priests, and prepare some of the materials used, such as oil and incense. The main contingent of 212 gatekeepers received reinforcements from the villages as needed.

Musicians (9:33–34)

Since David understood how important proper music was in worship, he installed professional musicians to advance that part of the service. This office continued. The musicians lived on the tabernacle grounds and had no obligations beyond being on call around the clock for musical duties. At this point the list of returning Levite families is finished.

■ *The chronicler demonstrated that the genea-*
■ *logical lines extended all the way to his con-*
■ *temporary audience, the people who had*
■ *returned from Exile. The Levites with all of*
■ *their divisions and duties were at the focus of*
■ *the return to rebuild the Temple.*

There were two large-scale returns from the Exile: the first one under Zerubbabel in 536 B.C. and the second one under Ezra in 459 B.C.

Saul's Line Again (9:35–44)

Except for some minor spelling differences, this list is identical with the one of 8:29–38.

QUESTIONS TO GUIDE YOUR STUDY

1. What contributions are made by each section of the genealogical lists?
2. What do we learn about the people of each tribe from these lists?
3. How do these lists contribute to the over-all purpose of Chronicles?

First Chronicles does not spend much time on King Saul. One gets the impression that his only role was to pave the way for David. But there is also further notice served in his brief treatment of the tragic king: The disaster of Saul's reign as a result of his unfaithfulness provides motivation for the steadfastness of David's monarchy. And it also helps to establish both positive and negative role models for Chronicles' original readers.

- *The negative picture of Saul prepares the*
- *way for the positive picture of David.*

SAUL'S LAST STAND (10:1–12)

Saul had come to power through military successes against the Philistines. Toward the end of his life, virtually all of his early victories were nullified by a resurgent Philistine army. The last battle took place in the northern part of Israel, just south of the Sea of Galilee. The Philistine army was clearly in the process of subduing a large part of Saul's kingdom.

This battle turned out to be a rout by the Philistines. The Israelite army fled. Saul's sons were killed, and then an arrow pierced Saul as well. Because Saul did not wish to fall into the hands of the uncircumcised Philistines, he asked his sword bearer to finish the job. When the loyal young man refused, Saul took his own life.

The Philistines discovered Saul's body the next day when they were stripping the bodies on the battlefield of their valuables. When they found Saul's corpse, they severed his head to display it

The Philistines were known as a "sea people." Originally at home in the fabulous civilization of early Crete, they expanded around the Mediterranean world through sea trade which led to the establishment of trading cities. The branch of this nation with which we are concerned had settled the tract of land along the coast between Judah and Simeon to the north and Egypt to the south. They flourished and attempted to expand their territory several times. The days of Samuel and Saul, as well as the early years of David, are characterizd by incessant warfare with the Philistines.

in the temple of Dagon, their god. The inhabitants of the town of Jabesh Gilead risked their lives to recover Saul's body and give him a decent burial.

Thus the reign of Saul, once the champion of God and Israel, came to a miserable end.

- *King Saul's death occurred in such a way*
- *that virtually everything he had accomplished in his life was undone.*

CHRONICLES' COMMENTARY ON SAUL (10:13–14)

The reader of Chronicles looks in vain for any expression of pity for Saul. The chronicler's commentary amounts to pointing out that Saul got what he deserved. There are four flaws pointed out: First, Saul was unfaithful to God when he disobeyed Him (1 Sam. 13:7–14). Second, Saul did not keep God's word when he obeyed God only partially (1 Sam. 15). Third, Saul consulted a medium (1 Sam. 28:7–25). Fourth, he did not seek guidance from God. The chronicler did not usually mind finding good in an otherwise evil person (see the words about the wicked king Manasseh in 2 Chron. 33:13). But the lessons of Saul's life were too poignant—the results of his disobedience too vivid—to gloss over. Chronicles' early readers who were receiving instructions on their heritage and duties were shown the grim side of God's call—the consequences of not obeying.

With particular calls from God come larger responsibilities. King Saul was obligated to lead his people spiritually as well as politically. Recall the words in James: those who teach will be judged more strictly than others (Jas. 3:1).

■ *The chronicler wanted us to realize that*
■ *Saul's demise was the direct result of his*
■ *unfaithfulness.*

QUESTIONS TO GUIDE YOUR STUDY

1. How did Saul's last day fit into his life up to then?
2. What were the specific points of disobedience that led to Saul's failure as person and as king?

THE REIGN OF KING DAVID (11–29)

The rest of this book devotes itself to King David. As mentioned at the outset, the chronicler does not put David's personal struggles in view. Thus, we learn nothing of the strife involving David's sons or the episode involving adultery with Bathsheba. Instead, the account in Chronicles remains zeroed in on David's public activity as head of his nation and thus as the one who was responsible for the spiritual welfare of the people as well.

- *The positive portrait of David provides a role*
- *model for the nation in Ezra's day.*

The account does include David's second major sin, the census, but this was a sin involving the entire nation, and it had consequences for all the people. On the whole, however, the reign of David is portrayed as a model for the people of God, united under a godly king, carrying out the required worship in a responsible and punctilious manner.

DAVID'S ANOINTING AS KING (11:1–3)

The chronicler picks up the story of David at the point at which David became king over all twelve tribes. Up to this point David had been king of Judah only, reigning from Hebron in central Judah. Now representatives from all of Israel united to make David king. They acknowledged the leadership role David had been playing in Israel's security all along. Their acclamation praised him as their kinsman,

In addition to God's appointed line of kings, there had been several pretenders. Abimelech, son of Gideon, had proclaimed himself king (Judg. 9), and Ishbosheth, son of Saul, also sought to retain his father's throne (2 Sam. 2).

The stronghold known as Jebus was the citadel of Jerusalem. This ancient site had been inhabited for a long time. A thousand years earlier, Abraham had encountered Melchizedek, the priest-king of "Salem" (Gen. 14:18). Among a number of clay tablets found in Amarna, Egypt, there are letters from the king of Jerusalem pleading to the pharaoh for help against invading marauders. These letters date roughly from the time of the Conquest under Joshua. During the Conquest, Jerusalem was subdued and a settlement was planted, but the citadel had never been captured until David's victory.

something that would not have been easy to say for a member of a competing tribe until they had brought themselves around to a genuine loyalty to David.

In order to legitimize the new king's enthronement, he and the people formed a "compact" or covenant. By becoming king, David committed himself to looking out for the welfare of his subjects. As God had done through Samuel earlier, the people now anointed David as king.

- David came to the throne with the unified
- support of the people.

CAPTURE OF JERUSALEM (11:4–9)

When David came to the throne, the citadel of Jerusalem was still inhabited by the Jebusites, who had no inclination to yield to the Hebrews. David's first act as king over all Israel was to capture the citadel, thereby finishing the work of the Conquest begun by Joshua. In the process, David accomplished two important measures:

1. He legitimated Joab as general of all his army when Joab found a way to take Jebus.
2. David set up Jerusalem as his new capital. Not only was it a highly defensible location, but it had not belonged to any tribe, so it was essentiallly neutral territory.

- David's capture of Jerusalem provided the
- setting for subsequent events, including the
- Temple in Solomon's day.

DAVID'S HEROES AND COMMANDERS (11:10–47)

Having reported on David's coronation, the chronicler paused to inform us of the men in David's army who occupied special positions.

The Three (vv. 10–19)

First, there was a group of three heroes, though only two names are given in this passage. Apparently the text in Chronicles (vv. 12–14) was miscopied by a scribe, who left out one of the three names and ran two episodes into each other. But with some help from 2 Samuel we can put the correct list together. Then we have: Jashobeam, who killed three hundred men at one time; Eleazar, who vanquished an entire army by himself in a barley field (2 Sam. 23:9–10); and Shammah, who defeated the Philistines in a lentil field (2 Sam. 23:11). These three heroes once risked their lives by penetrating behind enemy lines just to get David a drink of water, although David considered this water sacred and would not drink it.

The Two Leaders (vv. 20–25)

Two other men had distinguished themselves and become heroes. Abishai, a brother to Joab, had also killed three hundred people. He was not considered one of the legendary three above, but his fame was twice as great, and he was (at least in theory) their commander. Benaiah had a long list of exploits, including defeating two Moabite heroes, killing a lion, and defeating an Egyptian giant with the giant's own spear.

The Thirty (vv. 26–47)

Then there is the group of "thirty." Actually numbering thirty-seven, this list is a roll call of

Among the thirty heroes, two stand out: Asahel (v. 26), another brother of Joab, was killed by Abner, Saul's commander (2 Sam. 2). Uriah the Hittite (v. 41) was the husband of Bathsheba; he was sent to his death by David to cover up his adultery with her (2 Sam. 11).

other warriors who had distinguished themselves in David's service.

■ *Part of God's blessing on David was that he had*
■ *a strong army with many courageous men.*

MEN WHO RALLIED TO DAVID'S SIDE (12:1–22)

While the chronicler was on the subject of warriors, he compiled for us a representative register of military men who supported David before he became king.

David's Benjamite Supporters (vv. 1–7)

First we find a list of Benjamites who had forsaken their own tribesman, Saul, to support David in battle when David was at Ziklag in Philistine territory.

Gadite Supporters (vv. 8–15)

David received support from members of the tribe of Gad. These men came to David at the time of the spring floods when crossing the Jordan River was considered impossible.

More Supporters from Benjamin and Judah (vv. 16–18)

When another group composed of men from Judah and Benjamin came to David, he was suspicious. What did they have to gain by joining his cause? When David questioned this group, their chief, Amasai, was overcome by God's spirit, and he pledged his loyalty under divine inspiration.

Supporters from Manasseh (vv. 19–22)

It appears that some people who joined David's army did so, not so much out of support for David, as out of spite for Saul. Such must have been the case for the people from Manasseh, who joined David when he attempted to forge an alliance with the Philistines.

■ *David's later success as king was foreshad-*
■ *owed by the diverse people who joined his*
■ *cause.*

THE CORONATION PARTY (12:23–40)

Now our attention shifts again to the time of David's acclamation as king over all Israel while he was still holding court in Hebron of Judah. This event took place after the previous happenings around Ziklag and before David's capture of Jerusalem. A sizeable army, composed of more than three hundred thousand fighting men, descended on Hebron to anoint David. Of the numbers provided (none is given for Issachar except their chiefs, but see 7:5), by far the smallest was that for Benjamin, Saul's tribe, with only three thousand.

■ *David's reign began with a great celebration*
■ *attended by representatives for all of his*
■ *subjects.*

THE DISASTROUS FIRST ATTEMPT AT MOVING THE ARK (13:1–14)

Now that David had established himself as king over all of Israel in Jerusalem, he could continue to take the needed steps in governing a nation under God. Now David wished that the ark should be transported to Jerusalem and installed as the center of the worship of God.

During the years that David was in the wilderness hiding from Saul, he stayed in Philistine territory several times. Early on he spent some time in Gath (Goliath's home town!) pretending to be mad (1 Sam. 21:10–15). Later he came to Gath and was given the town of Ziklag. From there, he also carried out guerilla warfare against the Philistines (1 Sam. 27).

Usually, ancient armies would feed themselves through plundering and pillaging; in this case, that method was obviously unacceptable. For the sake of any reader worrying about how so many people could be fed by the little town of Hebron, the chronicler makes the point that they brought their own food and that the tribesmen from furthest north carried their provisions on pack animals. The emphasis on food also evokes images of a huge banquet, thus highlighting the festive nature of the occasion.

The symbol of God's presence among his people had become the ark, the ornate chest which contained the stone tablets with the Ten Commandments. The ark was also used as the focal point for receiving divine guidance (a mechanism which is now unknown to us). But the ark had fallen into disuse. The Israelites had attempted to use the ark as a talisman for victory against the Philistines, and God had allowed it to fall into the enemies' hands. When the ark brought a plague on the Philistines, they returned it. During the decades of Saul's rule, it had rested on the farm of Abinadab.

David conferred with a large assembly, and they all agreed enthusiastically.

When the day for moving the ark came, David and his associates made some fundamental mistakes. Numbers 4:15 provides explicit instructions for the transport of the ark. It was supposed to be carried by Levites bearing long poles on their shoulders, with these poles inserted into rings on the chest. The ark was never actually to be touched directly. Instead of following these directions, the people placed the ark on an oxcart and began the trek up the mountain to Jerusalem. What a day of jubilation it was! Some thirty thousand people played music, danced, cheered, and praised God in this procession.

Then suddenly there was stark, terrified silence. As the oxen trudged along, they hit an unevenness in the road and began to stumble; the ark almost slipped off the cart. One of the cart drivers, Uzzah, grabbed the ark to keep it from falling. As soon as he touched it, God killed him on the spot for violating the sanctity of the ark.

David was furious. In frustration, he aborted the attempt to move the ark up to Jerusalem and let it, instead, be taken to the homestead of Obed-Edom, who belonged to the line of the Levites (15:18; 26:4) and who was subsequently blessed by God's presence.

Although God is a God of grace, He is never to be taken lightly. In Acts 5:1–11, we read of Ananias and Sapphira, two people who were struck dead because they thought they could get away with lying to God.

■ *In spite of good intentions, David and his*
■ *company violated God's holiness with their*
■ *attempt at moving the ark.*

DAVID'S PROSPERITY (14:1–7)

Before resuming the story of the ark, the chronicler gives us a glimpse of David's lifestyle, now that he was rich and famous. Hiram, the king of Tyre, sought to buy David's favor by contributing to the building of a palace for the king of Israel. We also read of David's "other wives" (Bathsheba is not mentioned by name) and a list of his sons born in Jerusalem.

■ *David enjoyed God's material blessings.*

DEFEAT OF THE PHILISTINES (14:8–17)

The last century or so had seen warfare against the Philistines. At various times, each one had gained the upper hand. By the end of Saul's reign the Philistines had been able to subdue a large part of Israelite territory. Once David had come to the throne, this long-standing war reached a quick end. Two battles fought were in short succession, and they sealed the outcome. Apparently, the Philistines had spread themselves thin in carrying out raiding parties as well as searching for their old nemesis, David.

When David heard of the presence of the Philistines in the valley of Rephaim, he consulted God, and with the Lord's consent he led a frontal assault on the Philistine army. The rout was so extensive that the enemies left their idols on the battlefield, and David burned them.

Nevertheless, the Philistines attempted a return visit. They came to the same location on a raid, this time no doubt weary and prepared for a similar attack by David's forces. But David had again consulted God. "Do we do the same thing again, Lord?" he asked. "No," was God's reply,

This episode points out an important lesson, both for David and for us. If David had any notion that he could command God into his presence and build a relationship with God on David's terms, that idea was snuffed out for good. God manifested His holiness, teaching us that no matter how good He is and how much He blesses us, He is still God. He continues as holy and untouchable. Even the closest relationship with Him may not compromise His purity and His sovereignty.

Tyre was an ancient Phoenician city which had grown wealthy through extensive sea trade. Tyre consisted of two sections, a city on the shore and a citadel on an island in the sea. The former was probably first conquered by Nebuchadnezzar; the latter not until Alexander the Great built a causeway for his army to reach the island.

"this time you come from the rear. I will give you the signal; listen to my footsteps in the balsam trees" (cf. Ps. 68:7).

Thus, David's victory was to be God's victory first. David complied with God's instructions and won the battle. Verse 16 gives us in understated prose a remarkable military achievement: The entire land was liberated from the Philistines. And thereby, the kingdom of David became a superpower in the region in his day.

Humanly speaking, part of David's success was due to the relative weakness of traditional powers in the Fertile Crescent. Egypt, Babylon, and Assyria were occupied with their own internal problems at the time, and so the kingdom of David really was the strongest nation in the Middle East at that time.

■ *David's success as military leader is best seen*
■ *by his success against Philistia and his reli-*
■ *ance on God.*

PREPARATIONS FOR THE SECOND TRANSPORT OF THE ARK (15:1–24)

Once David had settled into his own quarters, he set out again to bring the ark to Jerusalem. But in the meantime he had done some research, so he knew how to do it correctly. First he prepared a tent to house the ark in Jerusalem. Then he called an assembly in Jerusalem to which he gave explicit instructions on how the ark was to be transported. David made sure that the priests and Levites were present. The chronicler could not pass up the opportunity to provide yet another list—this one of the Levitical families represented.

Then we read David's charge to the Levites: they were to carry the ark with poles on their shoulders just as God had directed. And they were not to do so unless they had first consecrated themselves for divine worship. In addition, David organized the music to provide singing and musical accompaniment. The four instruments played by this Levitical orchestra were the cymbal, the lyre, the harp, and the trumpet. The list of musicians included Asaph as always. Obed-Edom, whose actual job may have been as gate keeper, joined the orchestra. He, after all, had been host to the ark for the last few months.

- *The second attempt at moving the ark com-*
- *plied with biblical instructions. The Levites*
- *played a prominent role in its transport.*

THE SUCCESSFUL PROCESSION (15:25–29)

This time all went smoothly. With pomp and circumstance, the ark was transported from Obed-Edom's house to Jerusalem. No one incurred the wrath of God this time, and so the company sacrificed seven bulls and seven rams to thank God for their safety during this undertaking. David, however, did incur the wrath of Michal, his wife. Apparently David had gotten carried away by the exuberance of the moment. At first, David led the parade clothed in a robe, but by the time he got to Jerusalem, he was singing and dancing in nothing but his loin cloth (the ephod, an apron usually worn by priests). When Michal saw David make a spectacle of himself, she was thoroughly disgusted with him.

- *The ark was moved to Jerusalem. In spite of*
- *David's estrangement from Michal, it was a*
- *joyous day for him.*

Cymbals were percussion instruments. Lyres were hand-held stringed instruments, and harps were probably larger versions of the lyre. These would have been best suited for accompaniment. Trumpets would have been either ram horns or goat horns, providing a high, penetrating sound.

The burnt offering represented wholehearted devotion to God. A peace offering was a celebration of the covenant between God and His people (Lev. 1:1–14; 3:1–17).

Michal had little reason to like David by this point. Even though she had been in love with David at one time, Saul had offered her hand to David for a very fickle reason: Saul intended to find a way to have David killed. Michal's grizzly bride price was to be a hundred Philistine foreskins. But David survived the adventure and doubled the number of Philistines killed and trophies snatched in his eagerness to become the king's son-in-law (1 Sam. 18:17–29).

When strife with Saul broke out, David abandoned Michal, only to have her ordered back to him once he became king. (2 Sam. 3:14–16). By this time, Michal had married another man. And not too much later, David was at least indirectly responsible for the death of her brother Ishbosheth, who could have been king.

INSTALLATION OF THE ARK (16:1–3)

Having completed the procession up the mountain, David and the priests placed the ark inside the new tent of worship. Finally, order had been restored: The ark was in a tent in the new capital city. Burnt offerings and peace offerings comprised the dedication ceremony. At the close of the festivities, David treated each person to a small gift of food.

■ *The ark was placed in a tent, ready for wor-*
■ *ship of God.*

INSTALLATION OF LEVITES (16:4–6)

A group of Levites now received a charge to conduct public worship before the ark. While the other priests and their assistants conducted sacrifices at the altars, these men would furnish music and chanting. Two priests were in charge of blowing the trumpet in front of the ark.

■ *The worship around the ark was well*
■ *organized.*

DAVID'S DEDICATION PSALM (16:7–36)

The chronicler now reports on a psalm which David had written to commemorate the occasion. He gave it to Asaph, the chief musician, for performance.

The psalm which David composed for this occasion also became a part of some other psalms.

First Exhortation to Praise (vv. 8–13)

The exhortations to thank God and proclaim Him were grounded in two further exhorta-

1 CHRONICLES	PSALMS
16:8–22	105:1–15
23–33	96:1–13
34–36	106:1, 47, 48

Looking at the psalm as it is given in this context, we can discern the following pattern: There were four exhortations to praise God, connected by three passages detailing God's greatness. The pattern went like this:

8–13	Exhortation to Praise
14–22	God's Faithfulness
23–24	Exhortation to Praise
25–27	God's Glory
28–29	Exhortation to Praise
30–33	Praise from Creation
34–36	Exhortation to Praise

tions. The people were to *look to* God, and they were to *remember* His deeds. The biblical understanding of what it means to praise God does not consist of mindless repetition of words of flattery, but of rejoicing in the experience of God's closeness to Israel, both past and present.

God's Covenant Faithfulness (vv. 14–22)

David now gave reasons why God should be praised. He is the ruler (judge, v. 14) of the earth. As such, He kept the covenant that He made with His people—that the descendants of Abraham would possess the land of Canaan some day.

Second Exhortation to Praise (vv. 23–24)

The people of God were to proclaim to the nations what God had done. Their story was the story of a real and active God.

God's Unique Glory (vv. 25–27)

In distinction to the idols of the nations, God is the one who actually made the universe.

Third Exhortation to Praise (vv. 28–29)

The third call to praise was to "ascribe" to God what rightly belongs to Him. Here worship consisted of recognizing the attributes of God, specifically His glory and strength.

God Is Praised by the Created Order (vv. 30–33)

God's greatness was also invoked by the earth, which shook but did not fall, the heavens, the sea, the fields, and the trees of the forest. Their very existence as well as their constancy called attention to their Creator.

Fourth Exhortation to Praise (vv. 34–36)

This psalm concluded with a final call to praise, which also included a touch of petition. The people were enjoined to thank God and to praise God. They were also taught to call out to God for further divine acts of salvation. Although David was celebrating a high point in his life and the life of the nation, there still was no decisive peace in the world.

- David composed a psalm to praise God for all
- He had done as the ark came to Jerusalem.

CONCLUDING WORSHIP BEFORE THE ARK (16:37–43)

The chronicler clarifies at this point that in addition to the worship in Jerusalem, the tabernacle in Gibeon was still an active site of worship with the high priest Zadok and the musician Heman in charge. The account of the dedicatory service in Jerusalem concludes with the statement that everyone returned home. David, having experienced God's presence, went home to his palace to share the blessing with his family.

■ *The ark was installed in Jerusalem, but there*
■ *was no Temple yet. Worship continued at the*
■ *tabernacle as well as in Jerusalem.*

DAVID'S TEMPLE PLANS AND GOD'S PROMISE (17:1–15)

After an unspecified time, David began to make plans to build a house for God that would be at least as beautiful as his own palace. Initially Nathan the prophet encouraged him because he knew David to be a man of God. However, the next night God spoke to Nathan, canceling any plans David might have had. God's message to David through Nathan had these three points:

1. David's impetus for building a Temple did not come from God. God did not need a Temple (vv. 4–6).

2. God reminded David of all He had done for him and promised His continued blessing (vv. 7–10a).

3. God promised David that his son would build a Temple, and there would be a descendant of David on the throne of Judah forever (vv. 10b–14).

■ *God did not want David to build a Temple,*
■ *but He promised him that his descendants*
■ *would continue his royal line.*

Even though David had erected a tent in Jerusalem to house the ark, and even though there were sacrifices performed in and around it, this tent was not the same as the official tabernacle. The tabernacle was the highly ornate tent originally constructed by Moses and his associates at the command of God in the wilderness (Exod. 25–30). This tabernacle was to be the central place of worship—but not necessarily the only one—when the people first settled in the land. At the time of David, the tabernacle was still standing in Gibeon, although it had not contained the ark of the covenant for a hundred years.

This part of the prayer may strike us as peculiar. If God had promised to do this, why did David need to remind God of the promise, let alone beg God to keep His word? After all, when God speaks, does this not settle the matter? Or was God's keeping of the promise perhaps dependent on David's prayer to that effect?

The answer to this little puzzle teaches us something about the essence of prayer. Of course, God's keeping His word is not dependent on David's prayer. But prayer should not to be viewed as a means of getting God to do something He would otherwise not do. Prayer is a personal communication between God and the human person. The one who is praying should disclose to God everything that he feels and desires, even if it seems unnecessary.

God wants His children to open up to Him at all times. Thus, this prayer becomes an example of how closely David was walking with the Lord and how David was conforming his wishes and desires to God's

DAVID'S PRAYER (17:16–27)

Overcome by God's generosity, David said a prayer of gratitude.

David's Self-Awareness (vv. 16–19)

David felt overwhelmed by God's grace and mercy. It was God's love alone that made this shepherd boy a powerful monarch whose family would be the perpetual dynasty of the kingdom. What could David do but acknowledge himself as nothing more than God's servant and rejoice in God's goodness?

God's Greatness (vv. 20–22)

There is an interesting turnabout in this section of David's prayer. David exulted in God's magnificence. But this uniqueness also reflects on God's people, who give testimony to God's magnificence—not by their own greatness but by the fact of having been chosen by the Lord.

David's Plea for God's Constancy (vv. 23–27)

David concluded his prayer by moving from thanking God for what He had provided to entreating God to abide by His promise to bless David's descendants forever.

■ *In this prayer, David expressed his gratitude,*
■ *his amazement at God's goodness, and his*
■ *willingness to obey the Lord.*

THE GREATNESS OF DAVID'S KINGDOM (18:1–17)

In relatively few words, this chapter describes the grandeur of David's kingdom. Military conquests combined with booty and tributes established David as a powerful ruler in the Middle East. We read of David's accomplishments in succinct fashion. Some of these incidents are elaborated in later chapters.

Defeat of Various Nations (vv. 1–6)

Previously we read that David had driven the Philistines out of the land. Now we also see that David invaded the Philistines' territory and subdued them there.

A quick inventory of David's conquered territory reveals that God's promise to Abraham centuries before (Gen. 15:18) had been fulfilled: Abraham's descendants now occupied all the land from the Euphrates River in the north to the river of Egypt in the south. To the west, all the Philistine land was under Israelite domination, while to the east, on the other side of the Jordan River, the Moabites had been subjugated.

Tally of Tributes (vv. 7–11)

In this passage, the chronicler included a partial listing of some of the wealth that David accumulated through booty and tributes. Then as now, precious metals were important components of prosperity, and David received many objects of gold, silver, and bronze. David dedicated these to the Lord and His service. Some of the bronze went into Solomon's Temple project after David's reign was over.

Further Victory (vv. 12–13)

This section mentions the overwhelming victory of Abishai over the Edomites. Abishai, son of Zeruiah, is listed among the heroes of chapter 11 as the commander of the "three," though not actually one of them. Joab, his brother, was commander of David's army, and David, of course, was king; but apparently it was Abishai who really carried out the work.

The line of David continued on the throne of Judah without interruption until the Babylonian Exile. As we saw in the genealogy of chapter 3:17–24, official records continued the line of descent even after the Exile when there was no more throne. But God was faithful to His promise because Jesus Christ—the descendent of the house of Judah—is sovereign ruler on heaven's throne for all eternity.

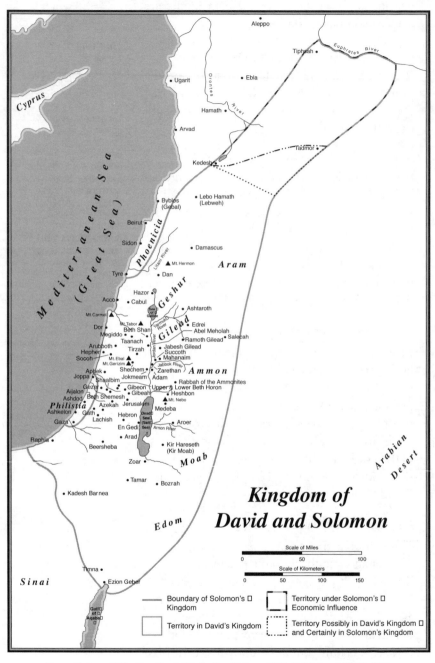

Kingdom of David and Solomon

From *Holman Bible Handbook* (Nashville: Holman Bible Publishers, 1992), 259.

The Top People (vv. 14–17)

Now follows another mention of the important people in David's reign. Once again we see Joab as the head of the army. Two men are listed as priests—Zadok and Ahimelech. Since we know that Zadok officiated in the tabernacle at Gibeon, it is possible that Ahimelech may have been the head priest before the ark in Jerusalem.

In charge of David's Cretan and Philistine bodyguards, the Kerethites and Pelethites, was Benaiah, whom we met in chapter 11 as the hero who killed an Egyptian giant with his own spear. We also note two important people in the administration of a kingdom the size of David's: Jehoshaphat was the official record keeper, and Shavsha was the secreatary—the person who maintained David's correspondence. Finally, David's sons are also mentioned as occupying positions of honor.

■ *David's greatness is shown by his impressive*
■ *military victories and administrative skills.*

WAR WITH THE AMMONITES AND THEIR ALLIES (19:1–20:3)

In this section, Chronicles provides further information on some of the wars waged by David. Most commentators agree that the episode with Ammon probably preceded the events of chapter 18.

Some Rash Decisions (vv. 1–5)

Nahash, king of Ammon, had apparently supported David in his wilderness days.

When Nahash died, his son Hanun came to the throne. David sent a mourning delegation to

The historical period of David falls into the so-called Iron Age; at this time functional articles, such as weapons and chariot wheels, were made of iron. The earlier ages were the Stone Age (prehistory), the Chalcolithic Age when things were made of copper (ca. 4500–3000 B.C.), and the Bronze Ages (Early, Middle, and Late, ca. 3000 B.C. to 1200 B.C.), when items were made of an alloy of copper and tin. Biblical history from Abraham to the judges took place in the Bronze Age. The Iron Age began shortly before the time of Saul; one way by which the Philistines kept Israel under control was by dominating iron production (1 Sam. 13:19–22).

There was a Nahash, king of Ammon, who with his insults had first caused Saul to take his kingship seriously as head of the Israelite army (1 Sam. 11:1). He may have been the father of the Hanan mentioned here.

Hanun to express sympathy, but Nahash, under the influence of some very poor advisors, humiliated David's ambassadors. David was outraged.

Preparations for Battle (vv. 6–9)

Realizing that David was deeply offended, King Hanun decided he needed to do something. And again he chose poorly. He formed an alliance with a number of his neighbors against Judah. And a massive army it was that he brought together! With the Aramean allies coming down from the north and the Ammonites lining up from the southeast, any Israelite army would be caught between these two lines.

Joab, commander of the Israelite army, realized the bind he was in. All he knew to do was to divide his army into two units, taking control of one half to go against the Aramean allies to the north, and putting his brother Abishai in charge of the other half to fight against the Ammonites to the southeast. Joab and Abishai made a pact to assist each other if either one of these forces were to get in trouble.

Humanly speaking, this was a pretty thin plan. But Joab, for all of his pragmatic ways, knew their fate was safely within the hands of God. He didn't know whether God would give him victory, but he knew that God would do whatever was best.

The Engagement: Stage 1 (vv. 14–15)

As it turned out, the victory was an easy one for the Israelites. The Aramean mercenaries were fighting not for their own interests, but for Hanun's silver. When the battle became difficult, they turned and fled before Joab and his troops. As soon as the Ammonites realized their supposed allies had deserted them, they also fled. Joab had attained his objectives, so he returned to Jerusalem.

The Engagement: Stage 2 (vv. 16–19)

Having fled from the Israelite army, the Arameans knew this would not be the end of the story. They immediately sought to reinforce themselves with further troops, even recruiting an army from beyond the Euphrates River. Hadadezer was the commander of this large force. This time David himself took charge of the Israelite army.

Perhaps Joab had returned to Jerusalem because the approaching winter rains would make moving an army across the Jordan River impossible. It could also be that it took David's personal authority to call an adequate army to meet the reinforced Aramean army.

David collected a massive force and crossed the Jordan River with them. This time it was a face-to-face confrontation between the two armies, and again David's army scored an overwhelming victory. At this point, the Arameans lost all taste for helping the Ammonites.

The Engagement: Stage 3 (20:1–3)

When spring came, Joab and David switched command again, and Joab led an army to subdue Ammon once and for all. With the taking of Rabbah, Joab and his troops scored a final victory. David presumably journeyed to the site of the triumph, where he was crowned with the massive crown of King Hanun.

Joab teaches us something about the nature of biblical faith. It is not a calculation of profits and losses. It is not an unreasoned optimism. It is trust in the person of God, Who is eminently trustworthy.

This was the time when David remained in Jerusalem and carried out his affair with Bathsheba. This chain of events culminated in David sending Uriah, Bathsheba's husband, to his death. Uriah was killed in this campaign at the siege of Rabbah, the capital of Ammon (2 Sam. 11). Chronicles skips this episode and simply focuses on the outcome of the war.

- David retaliated for the provocation from
- Ammon by defeating this country and its
- allies with the help of God.

DEFEAT OF THREE PHILISTINE GIANTS (20:4–8)

One group of giants was the Nephilim, who were the result of intercourse between the "sons of God" and "daughters of men" (Gen. 6:4). Other races of giants were among the people who instilled fear in the Israelites at the time of the wilderness wandering (Num. 13:28). The giants in the Philistine territory were descendants of these later strains.

There was another war with the Philistines, this time within Philistine territory. Three of David's men killed giants. Sibbecai, who was one of the thirty heroes, killed Sippai, the Rephaite; Elhanan slew the brother of Goliath; and David's brother Jonathan dispatched a twenty-four digited giant.

- David's military achievements were undergirded by the heroics of some of his men who
- slew giants just as he had done.

THE CENSUS AND ITS CONSEQUENCES (21:1–30)

In this chapter, we read of David committing a grave sin by taking a census of the fighting men. The whole country was punished with a plague. However, in the long run this misadventure had positive consequences because it resulted in David settling on the place where the Temple would be built.

The Census Taken (vv. 1–6)

God's law did not forbid a census. But one taken should be in conjunction with raising money for the service at the tabernacle. Otherwise, an epidemic would result (Exod. 30:11–16). Apparently David was interested in numbers so that he would know how large an army he had available. When he commissioned Joab to undertake this census, the pragmatic general was reluctant to do so, and he did not include the Levites or the Benjamites.

We read that this action was instigated by Satan, but we also know that it happened with God's consent, possibly as punishment for all the trouble Israel had caused David. (This may be implied by 2 Samuel 24:1, which follows the accounts of revolts by Absalom and others.)

Conviction and Punishment (vv. 7–15)

David realized he had done wrong (v. 7), but the message from the prophet Gad confirmed it. Of the three options of punishment, David chose three days of epidemic, fulfilling the warning of Exodus 30. Here as elsewhere in the Old Testament, the spread of the disease is pictured as carried out by an angel with a sword.

David at the Threshing Floor (vv. 16–30)

God commanded the angel to stop his work at the site of the threshing floor belonging to a Jebusite man named Ornan. David's palace was situated just south of this hill, and the king suddenly saw the angel. Immediately, David and his advisors entreated God to stop the plague. Shortly afterward, the prophet Gad brought word from God to David that he was to build an altar on that site. David encountered Ornan. Over Ornan's protests, David bought the property with a large sum of gold (preceded by a small downpayment of silver; 2 Samuel 24:24). The altar that he built was acceptable to God, and the epidemic stopped.

Satan does not appear often in the Old Testament. In Job 1 and 2 and in Zechariah 3:1, he functions as accuser against God's people. In these passages, he seems to have free access to God, and his opposition seems to be more to people than to God. A similar role is in view here in Chronicles: Satan attempted to bring about the downfall of David. Only in the New Testament do we see Satan's fully developed role as adversary to God as well as to the human race. Our understanding of Satan as a fallen angel in rebellion against God is based primarily on interpreting some Old Testament prophecies through the lens of some New Testament verses (see John 12:31; Rev. 8:10, 11; 12:7–9; 20:10 to clarify Isa. 14:12–14; Ezek. 28:12–14).

The threshing floor of Ornan was located on Mt. Moriah, adjacent to the fortification of Jerusalem, the place where Abraham displayed his faith in God by endeavoring to sacrifice Isaac (Gen. 22:1–14). Since the seventh century A.D. it has been the site of the Al Aqsa mosque and, shortly thereafter, the Dome of the Rock. The knights of the medieval crusade established a temporary headquarters here on the site of the Temple, for which they became known as the "Templars."

This principle applies today as then. It is easy to get so wrapped up in formal worship activity that we forget that God's primary interest is in our hearts and actions, not our ceremonies (Isa. 1:10–15).

■ *Contrary to the will of God, David took a cen-*
■ *sus. The result was an epidemic. In the course*
■ *of undoing his mistake, God showed David the*
■ *place where the Temple should be built.*

PREPARATIONS FOR THE TEMPLE (22:1–19)

While the tabernacle was still in Gibeon, David designated the threshing floor of Ornan as the site for the future Temple. He assembled much of the necessary material, and he charged Solomon and the people to pursue this project. Here we learn that David's record as a man of war prevented him from being the builder himself, while his son Solomon (the "man of peace") would have this privilege. David's exhortation to Solomon included the injunction that Solomon should be faithful to the Lord and obey His commands. The ceremonial worship of the Lord is always meaningless apart from personal devotion.

■ *Although he was not allowed to build the*
■ *Temple himself, David accumulated building*
■ *materials so that Solomon could do so more*
■ *easily.*

FIRST DESIGNATION OF SOLOMON AS KING (23:1)

When David was getting old, he made arrangements for a smooth transition after his death. First, he publicly declared that Solomon would inherit the throne from him, and was coregent from then on. As it turned out, this act was not accepted as final by several people, and it would have to be repeated twice more (1 Chron. 29:22; 1 Kings 1:38–39).

■ *David designated Solomon as his successor.*

ORGANIZATION OF THE PRIESTS AND LEVITES (23:2–24:31)

David also ensured continuity after his death by organizing the priestly families and all the duties of the Levites according to a fixed plan.

Review of Lineages and Duties (23:2–32)

What follows in chapter 23 reiterates some of the earlier material in 1 Chronicles, but it also adds a lot more detail and makes some changes. First, David took a (permitted) census of all of the Levites thirty years or older, subsequently changed to include those who were twenty and older. Of the thirty-eight thousand counted, twenty-four thousand were connected to the Temple, four thousand were designated as gatekeepers, four thousand as musicians, and six thousand as officials. Presumably, the latter group was in charge of enforcing the laws of purity. The rest of this chapter is given over to another list of the descendants of Levi and a brief enumeration of Levitical duties, with the one change that there was no longer any need for anyone to transport the ark. This detail is signaled in the text with the poignant phrase: "There was rest for the people" (v. 25). This condition, already foreshadowed in Joshua's day (Josh. 14:15), had found genuine fulfilment.

Twenty-four Shifts of Priests (24:1–19)

The number of priests among the sons of Levi had grown along with the rest of the tribe.

And yet there still was no true rest. In Hebrews 4:1–11, we read that true rest is found only on the basis of faith based on redemption.

Something needed to be done to make sure the priestly duties would be distributed fairly. Thus, David established twenty-four shifts among the priests, based on the families descended from Aaron's younger sons. The heads of the families drew lots to establish their order of serving. The families would rotate in ministering at the Temple according to this plan.

Zechariah, the father of John the Baptist, belonged to the shift of Abijah. He encountered an angel in the Temple when it was his division's turn to officiate (Luke 1:5).

Further Divisions Among Levites (24:20–31)

The Levites from the clans of Kohath and Merari were also divided by lots (v. 31), possibly again into twenty-four shifts. They were in charge of Temple support service.

■ *David arranged the priests and Levites into*
■ *divisions for effective service.*

TEMPLE MUSICIANS (25:1–31)

As we have seen, the author of Chronicles always pays close attention to the role of music in worship. The clans of Temple musicians also were divided into twenty-four shifts based on the families of Asaph, Jeduthun, and Heman, including 288 master musicians. Their duties involved songs and prophecies. David himself supervised this form of ministry.

In the Old Testament, prophecy is frequently connected to music. As the prophet's heart was soothed or inspired by the music, he was prepared to hear the word of God (1 Sam. 10:5; 2 Kings 3:15). Many Old Testament prophecies come to us in poetic or musical form.

■ *David paid particular attention to*
■ *well-arranged musical worship.*

GATEKEEPERS, TREASURERS, AND OFFICERS (26:1–32)

In this chapter, the other Levites and their divisions are presented.

Gatekeepers (vv. 1–19)

The gatekeepers were in charge of Temple security and propriety. Their rotations were set up in twenty-four divisions according to families as well.

Treasurers (vv. 20–28)

Over time, a lot of valuable things had been dedicated to God, and they needed to be stored in the Temple. The Levites were placed in charge of caring for these items.

Officers (vv. 29–32)

The Israelites now had a central government and a central house of worship. It was necessary to make sure that the laws of God would be maintained throughout the land. The officers' duty was to oversee matters of faith and purity. David divided them into west Jordan and east Jordan detachments.

■ *David made sure there were proper job*
■ *descriptions and work shifts for the staff of*
■ *the future Temple.*

THE ADMINISTRATION OF THE KINGDOM (27:1–34)

A kingdom as large as David's needed wise and efficient government with reliable subordinate officials.

The Army (vv. 1–15)

David maintained twelve divisions of the army, each totaling twenty-four thousand men, each on duty for a month. This arrangement had numerous benefits: There would be fresh troops on duty every month; soldiers could earn a living eleven months a year; and there would be no long-term standing army planning insurrections out of boredom. The list of commanders is drawn from chapter 11 where the heroes are enumerated.

Heads of Tribes (vv. 16–22)
Each tribe had an official administrator. This list comes out to twelve tribal heads, but only with some manipulation. For unknown reasons, Gad and Asher are not mentioned. There is a leader for Ephraim and two for each half of Manasseh. Aaron (the priestly line) has a special representative in addition to Levi, but should not be counted to make up the twelve.

The Census Again (vv. 23–24)
Once more the chronicler mentions the census of chapter 21. We are reminded that this census brought disaster. To compile a total census betrayed a lack of trust in God's promise of an uncountable nation.

Joab was David's nephew, the son of David's sister Zeruiah (1 Chron. 2:16). He is first mentioned in 2 Sam. 2 when he killed Abner to avenge his brother. Joab was a capable, rational man; he sent Uriah to his death (2 Sam. 11:1–25), killed Absalom (2 Sam. 18:11–15), and murdered his rival Amasa (2 Sam. 20:4–13). Upon David's death, he supported Solomon's rival, Adonijah, for which Solomon had him executed.

The Agricultural Cabinet (vv. 25–31)
King David appointed twelve men to oversee various aspects of the agricultural economy. The list of departments encompassed storage facilities, labor, and specific commodities.

David's Personal Advisors (vv. 32–34)
This list either supplements the list of 18:14–17 or supersedes it. No doubt in forty years of David's reign, there had been some replacements. The one constant was Joab, by now a grizzled veteran, who continued to be in charge of the army.

- David made sure there was an effective
- administration and bureaucracy to support
- his kingship.

THE TRANSITION TO SOLOMON AND DAVID'S LAST SPEECH (28:1–29:30)

The chronicler now resumes the historical narrative to finish the life of David and make the transition to Solomon. The setting was a special assembly called by David. All the main officials were summoned to be a part of the proceedings.

David's Speech (vv. 2–8)

David began the ceremony by recounting his plans to build a Temple and telling what God had said in response. The content parallels chapter 17.

David's Charge to Solomon (vv. 9–21)

David turned to Solomon and gave him specific instructions. First, he reiterated the need for total devotion to the Lord by emphasizing the relationship between seeking God and enjoying His presence. The price of not seeking was to be rejected. Then David presented Solomon with all the preliminary work he had done for the Temple: the blueprints, the materials, and the organization. All these, David could say with assurance, came from the Lord Himself.

The Call for an Offering (29:1–5)

Turning once again to the people, David mentioned all the valuable resources he had devoted to the building of the Temple. And further, he announced another huge donation. This generosity was to encourage the assembly to respond with their offerings.

The People's Response (vv. 6–9)

David's listeners reacted by giving to this cause themselves. The telling commentary here is that they gave willingly (v. 6) and that the willingness of those who gave caused great rejoicing (v. 9).

David's Prayer (vv. 10–19)

We should never think that we can give God something that He does not already own. Giving is a matter of consecrating what God has entrusted to us to His use.

The prayer by David at the conclusion may be the last piece of poetry he ever wrote. It began with David's affirmation of God's ownership of all creation.

Second, David confessed his own unworthiness. Third, he placed before God his own integrity and that of the people in making the offerings. Fourth, David closed the prayer by entreating God to preserve this attitude of devotion and to maintain Solomon in obedience to the divine commandments.

Solomon's Coronation (vv. 20–25)

The assembly adjourned for the day after David had led in the praise and worship of God. But it came together again the next day for two important ceremonies. First, there was a sacrifice of thousands of animals to God and its feast. The sacrifice was followed by a second anointing and enthronement of Solomon as king. The chronicler ignores the complications recorded in 1 Kings 1 and 2 and tells us the end result: Solomon began his reign as ruler of Israel with the support of the people, but, even more importantly, the blessing of the Lord.

Close-out of David (vv. 26–30)

The author of Chronicles rounds out his portrait of David with a quick summary. David had reigned forty years, and his long life ended with prosperity and esteem. He left Solomon a grand legacy.

■ *David commended the kingdom to his son*
■ *Solomon. This charge included particularly*
■ *the Temple project and instructions to*
■ *remain obedient to the Lord's word.*

QUESTIONS TO GUIDE YOUR STUDY

1. What traits of David made him such a good king?
2. How were David's walk with God, administrative success, and military success related?
3. What were the various features of David's reign that could have served as a model for the people in Ezra's day?

THE REIGN OF SOLOMON (2 CHRONICLES 1–9)

Solomon means literally "Man of Peace." His birth name was Jedidiah, "Beloved of the Lord," and this name was bestowed on him by God Himself (2 Sam. 12:24–25). Both of these names are characteristic of Solomon. God loved him and appointed him for his kingship from his conception on, and his forty-year reign was remarkable for its peace.

Although there is no physical evidence for this claim, many people believe that originally 1 and 2 Chronicles were one scroll, eventually divided for convenience's sake. Thus, the narrative would have continued without a break from the death of David into the reign of Solomon. For the chronicler, Solomon was the man of the Temple pure and simple. The entire account focuses on the building of his Temple and its glory. All of Solomon's other accomplishments are derived from his faithfulness as Temple builder. As with David, we learn nothing of his personal struggles or of the sin which brought about his punishment in the latter years of his reign (1 Kings 11:1–40). We see only the man who was faithful to God in building the Temple and how God blessed him as a result.

- Solomon continued the chronicler's picture
- of the ideal role model for his day. He was a
- man of peace and glory, brought about by his
- devotion to building the Temple.

SOLOMON'S ESTABLISHMENT AND VALIDATION (1:1–17)

Once Solomon was settled on the throne, he had the loyalty of the entire kingdom. The rivalry of which we read in 1 Kings 1 and 2 was confined to his own family; there were no rivals outside of Judah contending for the throne. He confirmed his rule by calling for an assembly at the tabernacle at Gibeon—still the main place of worship. There he performed a monumental sacrifice. An altar dating all the way from the time of Moses was still in use there.

Solomon's Vision (vv. 7–12)

Without any further explanation of the process, the chronicler tells us that God appeared to Solomon that night and granted Solomon a wish. The new king, overcome by his sense of responsibility, asked for one thing: the wisdom to govern the people properly. God was pleased with Solomon's request. He did not ask for material things or selfish things like glory and honor. God rewarded Solomon for his request by giving him the wisdom he asked for as well as all the things he did not ask for—wealth, honor, and glory.

Validation: Solomon's Wealth (vv. 13–17)

Upon his return to Jerusalem, Solomon ruled in grand style. Solomon's wealth encompassed luxuries such as gold, silver, cedar wood, and military items, including horses and chariots. Utilizing the kingdom's strategic position at the center of the Fertile Crescent, Solomon was able to control trade to his advantage, such as reselling horses from Egypt to the Hittites at a considerable profit. In those days the worthiness of an army was based on its chariot corps, and Solomon had more than enough.

■ Solomon came to the throne with the blessing
■ of God. He worshiped the Lord and received
■ the Lord's validation in a vision and in mate-
■ rial success.

The main altar at the tabernacle was made of acacia wood overlaid with bronze. Its dimensions were three cubits by five cubits long and wide (Exod. 27:1). In contrast, the altar made by Solomon was ten cubits tall by twenty cubits long and wide. A cubit equals approximately 18 inches. Thus, Solomon's altar would have required steps to make it usable.

Solomon's request points out an important consideration for us in our prayers. It is not that we should not ask for material things if we need them. But it is more important that we desire those things which reflect the work God is doing with us—molding us to the image of Christ and preparing us for a specific calling. We should not generalize from Solomon's example that every time we ask for something within God's will, He will also give us rewards.

Although chariots had been in use at least since the days of Abraham, they did not really become practical until the Iron Age. From that era on, they constituted the "armored units" of any army. Solomon distributed his chariot divisions in strategic cities around the kingdom.

Hiram was king of Tyre for thirty-four years, overlapping the reigns of David and Solomon. He was able to maintain cordial relationships with both Hebrew rulers. According to tradition, Hiram and Solomon amused themselves by wagering on problems they sent each other to solve.

BUILDING PREPARATIONS (2:1–18)

It may be as difficult to keep a kingdom as to acquire it. How does one keep the people unified when there are no more enemies to fight? Solomon did so with extensive, lifelong building projects. The most important work was the construction of the Temple. The actual hard labor was done by 150,000 aliens living in the land who were conscripted by Solomon to this purpose; these men were supervised by 3,600 Israelites. Even though David had already made far-flung preparations, Solomon needed far more building materials to suit his grandiose plans. To this end he set up a contract with King Hiram of Tyre.

Solomon's Letter (vv. 3–10)

Solomon requested two things from Hiram: wood, particularly cedar, but also other varieties, and a skilled artisan who could supervise the entire building projects. In the process he explained to Hiram the nature of the building—that it would be a Temple to serve the God of Israel. But he made a particular point to Hiram in order to clarify something which Hiram, as a pagan, might not understand. Hiram ought not to think that somehow the presence of God was restricted to the Temple. God does not need houses in which to live.

Hiram's Reply (vv. 11–15)

Hiram recognized a good business deal when he saw it, and he confirmed Solomon's order. With complimentary remarks about both God and Solomon, he sent the required materials by sea to Joppa. From there the Israelites had to transport them about forty miles inland and uphill. Hiram also sent a master builder named Huram, who was of Israelite ancestry. Huram was probably knowledgeable about the Jewish culture as well.

- *Solomon received building material from*
- *King Hiram. But he made sure the pagan*
- *king knew about the distinctiveness of the*
- *God for whom the Temple was built.*

BUILDING THE TEMPLE (3:1–4:22)

In compliance with God's instructions through his father David, Solomon built the Temple on the threshing floor of Ornan on Mt. Moriah, just north of the palace. The information given in these two chapters is enough to give us a general picture of the Temple. But it is not enough to allow us to build an exact model of the Temple.

The Building (3:3–15)

To understand the nature of the Temple in all of its time periods, we must keep in mind that it always had two components: the actual roofed building and the open air courts surrounding it. The building itself was divided into two sections known as the Holy Place and the Most Holy Place. The main altar stood in front of the building in the innermost court. This basic plan was also the blueprint of the tabernacle. Other than the obvious points that Solomon replaced the tent with a firm structure and that he provided elaborate decorations, Solomon's innovation for the building were these:

1. He roughly doubled the size of the building compared to the tent.
2. He made a porch at the entrance of the building, possibly of towering height (vv. 3–4).

When Stephen, the first martyr for Christ, made his speech before the council, he suggested that his contemporaries' attachment to the Temple was similar to the worship of the golden calf in the wilderness. Jesus said to the Samaritan woman at the well that true worship is not tied to a building but is rooted in truth and spirit (John 4:24).

3. He placed two pillars in front of the entrance. Solomon gave these pillars the names Jakin and Boaz.

4. He provided two courts: an inner court and an outer court.

The inside of the building was lined with cedar wood, which is known for its durable quality, and then covered with gold. The Most Holy Place was dominated by two gilded cherubim, their wings covering the entire wall.

The Furnishings (4:1–22)

The main object used in worship was the altar. However, from what we read, the most eye-catching object was the "sea," a large basin resting on replicas of the heads of bulls. The sea, which stood to the left of the altar, was to be used by priests to cleanse themselves. (Sacrificing animals is grimy business.) On the other side were ten basins intended for ritual cleansings. Inside the Holy Place stood ten tables for the showbread and ten lampstands, five on each side.

Cherubim were one of the orders of angels present at the throne of God guarding His holiness. They were the sentries of the garden of Eden, and they were represented on the ark of the covenant in the curtain of the tabernacle, as well as in the Most Holy Place of the Temple. They are believed to have been lion-shaped with human faces and wings.

■ *Solomon's Temple was large and ostentatious.*
■ *The dimensions of the tabernacle were greatly*
■ *exceeded. He installed lavish furnishings.*

THE TEMPLE DEDICATION (5:1–7:22)

Solomon arranged for a big dedication ceremony. The three chapters in this section encompass four central components of the feast: moving in the ark, Solomon's sermon, Solomon's public prayer, and a weeklong celebration of the Feast of Tabernacles.

Solomon's Temple

From *Holman Book of Biblical Charts, Maps, and Reconstructions* (Nashville: Holman Bible Publishers, 1993), 142.

Moving in the Ark (5:1–14)

Once the building was finished and the furnishings were in place, one final task remained: to move the ark into the Temple. This event would signal the beginning of a new era. From now on the people of Israel would worship in a permanent place. Solomon called a large convocation of people who would be a part of the ceremony. Then the ark was officially relocated one more time. The procession moved from Mt. Zion, adjacent to Mt. Moriah, to the Temple. Priests carried the ark in the prescribed manner and left the poles attached to the ark—for what else could one possibly do with the implements that had been used to carry God's ark?

Originally the ark of the covenant contained three items: the tablets of the Law, a jar of manna (Exod. 16:33), and Aaron's rod that budded when the people grumbled (Num. 17:1–10). We are reminded of them by the author of Hebrews (9:4). By Solomon's time, only the tablets were left.

The celebration was accompanied by sacrifices in which all priests participated. All the musicians played, still led by the aging Asaph, Heman, and Jeduthun. The crowd chanted the single refrain: "God is good; His loving kindness endures forever!" Then, suddenly, God manifested Himself directly in a cloud. A large cloud started to fill the Temple. The cloud grew bigger and bigger until the priests—who would have been in the court of priests—could no longer carry on. Everyone understood that this cloud was the very glory of God Himself, just as God's glory had first filled the tabernacle in the days of Moses and Aaron (Exod. 40:34).

The glory of God was later called His "shechinah," which literally means God's "residence." It appeared to the Israelites at the Temple dedication, just as it had first filled the tabernacle in the days of Moses and Aaron (Exod. 40:34). Through this sign the people could know that God had taken up residence.

Solomon's Sermon (6:1–11)

In a short speech, Solomon reminded the people again of what had led up to this occasion. For the more than four hundred years that they had been in the land (1 Kings 6:1), there had been no permanent Temple. Now, by God's grace, there was one. Solomon emphasized what a privilege this was for Jerusalem, for the house of David, and for Solomon personally.

Solomon's Public Prayer (6:12–40)

Solomon saw himself as spiritual representative as well as political leader of his people. With dramatic flair, he stood in front of the sanctuary and raised his hands to heaven. Then he mounted a platform, came to his knees, raised his hands again, and spoke a prayer on behalf of all Israel. The prayer included the following items:

1. He reiterated God's graciousness in allowing the family of David to enjoy His blessings (vv. 14–15).

2. He pleaded for God to keep His promises to David as long as his descendants obeyed God (vv. 16–17).

3. He recognized that the Temple could not contain God, but that God had graciously made His presence available to the people. Solomon made reference to this truth throughout the rest of the prayer (vv. 18–21).

4. There followed several scenarios in which Solomon entreated God to answer from heaven if people prayed to Him (vv. 26–39):

   a. in case of a man being accused of a crime, so that God would reveal the guilt or innocence of the person if he prayed at the Temple (vv. 21–23);

   b. in case of defeat in war due to sin (vv. 24–25);

   c. in case of drought due to sin (vv. 26–27);

   d. in case of disasters due to the sin of various individuals (vv. 28–31);

   e. in case a foreigner wished to worship God (vv. 32–33);

In his prayer, Solomon acknowledged there was no human being who had not sinned, thereby foreshadowing the apostle Paul's words, "All have sinned and fall short of the glory of God" (Rom. 3:23). The closer we live to the presence of God, the more we are aware of our sinful state. Yet we also know Paul's sentence immediately afterward that we "are justified freely by his grace through the redemption that came by Christ Jesus" (Rom. 3:24).

The Temple dedication coincided with the Feast of Booths. The date given in verse 10 was the last official day of the feast prescribed in Leviticus 23:34. This holiday commemorated the Israelites' wanderings in the wilderness—an appropriate way to celebrate the fact that God's sanctuary now had a permanent home in Jerusalem.

f. in case the Israelites had been commissioned by God to undertake a military action (vv. 34–35);

g. in case the people sinned and had been punished by exile (vv. 36–39).

5. Solomon made an invocation to God to bestow His loving presence (vv. 40–42).

The Feast of Tabernacles (7:1–10)

God does not always answer our prayers in direct, visible fashion, but He did so for Solomon. At the close of Solomon's prayer, God sent fire from heaven to ignite the sacrifical offerings that had been put in place. Again the cloud of God's glory filled the premises, and again, the people continued to praise God. Meanwhile, Solomon prepared a second round of sacrifices consisting of forty-two thousand animals, which were to be eaten by the multitude. The altar was insufficient to hold this many animals, so Solomon had the priests use the bare ground in front of the sanctuary. Finally the celebration was over, and Solomon dismissed the people to their homes.

■ *Solomon dedicated the Temple with sacri-*
■ *fices, a speech, a public prayer, the Feast of*
■ *Booths, and more sacrifices. God validated*
■ *all these actions by displaying His glory.*

GOD'S SECOND APPEARANCE TO SOLOMON (7:11–22)

Years before, God had visited Solomon at night in the tabernacle at Gibeon. Now that the Temple project was complete, Solomon received another appearance from God. This time God confirmed privately everything that had been said before publicly. Specifically God stated that He did accept the Temple and that He would respond to prayer in the kinds of situations mentioned by Solomon in his prayer (vv. 13–16).

God also promised that He would follow through on His promise to David always to keep a descendant of David on the throne so long as the king followed God's commandments (vv. 17–18). Furthermore, God indicated He would punish the nation (the Hebrew "you" is plural) severely if they forsook the Lord and committed idolatry. God would reject this Temple and let His people be led into exile (vv. 19–22).

■ *God appeared again to Solomon and con-*
■ *firmed all that He had promised to David and*
■ *all that Solomon had asked for.*

SOLOMON'S GRANDEUR (8:1–9:31)

In 2 Chronicles, the description of Solomon's greatness frames a section which displays Solomon's faithfulness in carrying out all the sacrifices at the Temple. Clearly, the chronicler wanted us to see an unmistakable cause-and-effect relationship between Solomon's devotion and his success.

Solomon's Might (8:1–11)

The king carried out many building and renovation projects. We also receive a brief notice of Solomon subduing the kingdom of Hamath, his only known military expedition (v. 3). Chronicles does not dwell on Solomon's many marriage alliances except to mention his marriage to the daughter of Pharaoh—and then only to show that Solomon respected the holy places

In verse 14 we have the well-known reassurance from God: "If my people, who are called by my name, will humble themselves and pray and seek my face and turn from their wicked ways, then will I hear from heaven and will forgive their sin and will heal their land." We must not forget that God said this first of all to His chosen people, Israel, but we may also apply the principle to ourselves: God will respond to sincere repentance.

The chronicler mentions in verse 2 some towns which King Hiram of Tyre had given to Solomon. We know from 1 Kings 9:10–14 that these were villages which Solomon had originally awarded to Hiram. But Hiram passed them right back to Solomon because they were so dilapidated.

enough not to let his pagan wife live in their proximity (v. 11).

Solomon's Faithfulness in Temple Worship (vv. 12–16)

In this passage, we are reminded again that Solomon was meticulous in all his observances at the Temple. The chronicler enumerates the king's obligations and how he kept them in compliance with David's intentions.

Sea Trade (vv. 17–18)

The list of Solomon's accomplishments continues with his visit to the very southern end of his kingdom, Eloth on the north coast of the Red Sea. Solomon purchased a fleet of trading ships and their crews from Hiram, and he used these ships to increase his gold supply.

Visit from the Queen of Sheba (9:1–12)

Solomon's riches and wisdom had become so well known that the Queen of Sheba traveled to Jerusalem to find out the truth of the matter for herself. Although trade or a political alliance may have been part of her motivation, personal curiosity may have been the most important reason why she took this journey. She found Solomon to be extremely wise; his wealth and power had been understated. Although she brought extravagant gifts for Solomon, she went home with even more presents than she brought. (The chronicler is reminded at this point—verses 10, 11—of some other imports Solomon had garnered.) The centerpiece of this episode was the queen's declaration that all of Solomon's grandeur was the result of God's blessings (vv. 5–8).

Solomon's Great Wealth (9:13–28)

Solomon's wealth was incredible by the standards of any age or culture. His regular revenues were approximately forty tons of gold. Much of

The queen of Sheba ruled over the kingdom of the Sabeans, who enjoyed a flourishing culture. Saba occupied the southwestern corner of the Arabian peninsula, largely coinciding with the present country of Yemen. This area's long-standing history as the gateway to the east for trade in spices and incense lasted until the time of the Spanish and Portuguese explorers in the fifteenth century.

it was stored in the form of shields. Solomon's throne was an exercise in unrestrained luxury. The wealth of the ruler also trickled down to his subjects. Silver became almost worthless as a commodity because there was an overabundance of gold. The chronicler reiterates the point made in connection with David—namely, that during this time the kingdom covered the expanse of land promised to Abraham (v. 26; see also Gen. 15:18).

Solomon's Death (vv. 29–31)

Chronicles does not mention how Solomon's entanglements with pagan wives led to his downfall in God's eyes. The book leaves Solomon at the height of his glory because in this way, he was an example to the readers of the account in Ezra's time. Solomon was buried beside David. Throughout this book, the manner of a king's burial becomes an important indicator of how esteemed he was.

■ *Solomon's successes were the direct result of*
■ *his faithfulness. God demonstrated to the*
■ *world how obedience to Him paid off through*
■ *Solomon's wealth and splendor, particularly*
■ *as exemplified in the visit from the queen of*
■ *Sheba.*

QUESTIONS TO GUIDE YOUR STUDY

1. How did Solomon continue, advance, or depart from the model of David?
2. How was Solomon's success directly correlated to his faithfulness to God?
3. How was the Temple representative of God's relationship to human beings in its functioning and in its furnishings?

THE KINGS OF JUDAH (2 CHRON. 10–36)

Under Solomon's successor, his son Rehoboam, the nation split into the two kingdoms—Israel in the north and Judah in the south. The rest of this book consists of a survey of the kings of the Southern Kingdom from Rehoboam to the Exile. The chronicler ignored the simultaneous events in the north except where they impinged directly on the events in Judah. Even where this was the case, he assumed that his readers had some prior knowledge of the northern kings, perhaps from the accounts in 1 and 2 Kings.

As the history of the Southern Kingdom unfolds in 2 Chronicles, we see several constants emerge:

1. The kingdom of Judah had only one dynasty—namely the descendants of David.
2. There was a direct correlation between a king's obedience to the Lord and God's blessings on him and the kingdom.
3. When there were times of revival, the priests and the Temple played a leading role.

■ *God's work in history continued with the*
■ *Southern Kingdom (Judah), its kings, and its*
■ *Temple.*

REHOBOAM (10:1–12:16)

Because of his foolish arrogance, Rehoboam lost the ten northern tribes. Nevertheless, we see in Chronicles that Rehoboam was not a total

Kings of Judah

Name	Dates	Reference	Commentary
Rehoboam	931–913	10:1–12:16	division, some apostasy
Abijah	913–911	13:1–22	victory over Jeroboam
Asa	911–870	14:1–16:14	good, but departed slowly
Jehoshaphat	873–848	17:1–20:37	reforms, alliance with Ahab
Jehoram	848–841	21:1–20	evil, disintegration
Ahaziah	841	22:1–9	evil, killed by Jehu
Athaliah	841–835	22:10–12	daughter of Ahab,usurper
Joash	835–796	23:1–24:27	boy king, good for a time
Amaziah	796–767	25:1–28	compromise, held hostage
Uzziah	792–740	26:1–23	success, pride, leprosy
Jotham	750–731	27:1–8	very good
Ahaz	735–715	28:1–27	very evil
Hezekiah	729–686	29:1–32:33	extremely good, like a second Solomon
Manasseh	696–642	33:1–20	very evil, but repented
Amon	642–640	33:21–25	very evil, assassinated

Kings of Judah

NAME	DATES	REFERENCE	COMMENTARY
Josiah	640–609	34:1–35:27	thorough reforms
Jehoahaz	609	36:1–3	deposed by Neco, exiled
Jehoiakim	608–598	36:4–7	first deportation
Jehoiachin	598	36:8–9	second deportation
Zedekiah	598–587	36:10–13	destruction and third deportation

failure as a king. Ruling from Jerusalem, he remained the protector of the Temple and the true worship of God. In spite of a period of apostasy and punishment, his repentance brought relief.

Rehoboam's Arrogance and Its Consequences (10:1–19)

Solomon had used Israelite forced labor by the end of his reign. So when Rehoboam became king, a group of representatives came to him with an understandable demand—they wanted him to lessen the burden. The king asked for and was given three days to think it over. At the end of the period, this weak and unimaginative ruler repeated the formula that his younger advisers had coached him to say. This brought on an immediate crisis. The representatives of the ten northern tribes rejected Rehoboam with the same intensity with which their counterparts had sworn loyalty to David seventy-three years earlier (1 Chron. 11:1–2). Rehoboam barely managed to escape with his life, but Adoniram, the supervisor, was not so lucky.

The king returned to Jerusalem to govern Judah and Benjamin—the two tribes which remained faithful to him. The passage insists that in the final analysis, what happened was brought about by God, just as the prophet Abijah had warned Solomon that the ten northern tribes would secede. God was in charge of events, even if they included sinful human actions.

Rehoboam's Entrenchment (11:1–22)

Rehoboam's reaction was to try to coerce the ten northern tribes back under his control by means of military force. But God did not want this done, and through the prophet Shemaiah He let Rehoboam know His will. Rehoboam listened and obeyed.

Joseph told his trembling brothers in Egypt, "You intended to harm me, but God intended it for good to accomplish what is now being done, the saving of many lives" (Gen. 50:20). Although it may seem to us at times that God is only a spectator on the human scene, he has not let go of the reins of control.

Jeroboam, the new king of Israel, was doing everything in his power to fortify his position. Because Jerusalem housed the Temple and could possibly become an enticement for his subjects to return their allegiance to Judah, Jeroboam created new religious centers in Israel. He designated a new order of priesthood that would conduct the service at these new centers. As a result, priests and Levites from all over the Northern Kingdom came to Judah to take up residence in Jerusalem by the Temple, thereby strengthening Rehoboam's position.

A calf may seem like an odd object of worship. Would not a bull, a symbol of strength, be more appropriate? This question ignores the crucial role that the concept of fertility played in an agrarian society. A calf symbolized the renewal of life and provision for the community. Thus, the Israelites concocted a golden calf—the model of which had been erected before at Sinai (Exod. 32), and Jeroboam renewed this cult.

Rehoboam also undertook several other measures in order to contain the damage. He transformed a number of surrounding villages into fortifications, and he settled his sons throughout the remaining kingdom. His son Abijah received the title of heir apparent. By implementing these measures, Rehoboam managed to prevent any further insurrections.

Rehoboam's Faithlessness and Punishment (12:1–15)

Rehoboam was in a strategic position as guardian of the Temple and protector of the true worship of God. With the blessings of God, he enjoyed the first three years of his reign. But as soon as he became strong and prosperous, he turned away from God toward Canaanite worship (1 Kings 14:23–24). At least a part of this apostasy was due to the influence of Rehoboam's wife, Maacah, who propagated idolatry right into the time of Asa, her grandson (2 Chron. 15:16). As a result, God allowed Pharaoh Shishak of Egypt to invade the land.

Even though Shishak did not conquer Jerusalem (see below), he did carry off the shields of gold and other treasures that Solomon had accumulated. Rehoboam had to replace them with shields of bronze, and he had them heavily guarded at all times. Lest Rehoboam should misinterpret the message in these events, Shemaiah, the prophet, explained that this invasion was a direct punishment from God for Rehoboam's disobedience. Rehoboam understood, and he and the leaders repented. Shemaiah announced that God had accepted the repentance and that Jerusalem would be spared. Nevertheless, Chronicles' overall assessment of Rehoboam is negative because the king enticed the people to apostasy.

Part of the reason why David and Solomon (as well as Tyre and Philistia) were to grow strong in the Middle East was because there were no strong empires in Egypt or Mesopotamia. But those days were over. Egypt had a new, strong dynasty, founded by Sheshonk I, known in the Bible as Shishak. This pharaoh left records of his conquests on a stele found at Megiddo and in inscriptions at Karnak, Egypt. Shishak's mummy was found in 1938–39.

■ *Rehoboam was a weak king. According to*
■ *God's plan, he brought about the division of*
■ *the kingdom, but he was faithful enough to*
■ *maintain proper worship at the Temple.*

ABIJAH (13:1–22)

Chronicles does not point out Abijah's idolatry (1 Kings 15:3), but shows him at his best—the defender of God's kingdom. Some minor armed conflicts with Jeroboam's troops had occurred during Rehoboam's reign, but God had forbidden an all-out war. However, now it came to a major battle. Perhaps Abijah thought he could reunite the kingdom. Two large armies confronted each other: Abijah's four-hundred thousand men versus Jeroboam's eight-hundred thousand warriors. The location was close to the border between the two kingdoms.

In a manner typical of ancient times, Abijah made a speech to demoralize the northern army. The focus of his address was the Temple and the worship of God. He pointed out derisively how Jeroboam had invented a new pay-as-you-go priesthood, but that the true religion of the Lord was practiced faithfully in Jerusalem (a bit of hypocrisy on Abijah's part, in light of what we learn of him in 1 Kings 15:3).

While Abijah was making his speech, a contingent of Jeroboam's forces deployed themselves behind the southern army. When the battle began, Abijah was caught between an army twice the size of his. But because the southern army put their trust in God, He aided them, and they beat the overwhelming odds. Abijah was able to capture some of Israel's border towns; Jeroboam died in disgrace not much later. But neither did Abijah live much longer past this moment of glory. His reign lasted only three years.

- ■ *The faltering reign of Abijah had its high*
- ■ *point in the victory over the Northern King-*
- ■ *dom because Abijah trusted the Lord.*

ASA (14:1–16:14)

The compromising days of Rehoboam and Abijah were followed by the reign of Asa, a good and worthy king. Asa's reign was outstanding because of his commitment to the service of the Lord. Nevertheless, in his later years his devotion to God waned, and his reign also ended on a sour note.

Asa's Faithfulness and Success (14:1–8)

The chronicler lavishes high praise on Asa. This king showed a full commitment to God. He set out to eliminate all pagan worship from his kingdom. All pagan altars and images were to be destroyed (although apparently not all of Asa's lofty goals were attained; see 15:17). As a result, Asa was blessed with peace. Nevertheless, Asa also made sure that his towns were bulwarked, and that he had a fully equipped army—perhaps to be prepared for another invasion similar to Shishak's.

Zerah's Invasion (vv. 9–15)

The invasion did come. Zerah, an Ethiopian who may have been a king in his own right or a general for the pharaoh, invaded Palestine with a large army. But in contrast to Shishak's success against Rehoboam's weak forces, Zerah came against a much stronger enemy—the Lord Himself. Because of Asa's faithfulness, God granted Judah an overwhelming victory. Asa was able to drive Zerah's forces back, even beyond the original border, so that the army of

"High places" were worship sites erected on hills. They were frequently devoted to Canaanite idols, such as the god Baal. However, they could also be illegitimate places for worship of God. For example, today one can visit the remains of a scaled-down version of the Temple which had been set up at Arad in the Negev desert. The law specified that, once there was a designated place of worship, all other sites would be unacceptable (Deut. 12:26–27). Thus from Solomon's time on, only the Temple in Jerusalem was to be used for worship of God.

Judah was able to plunder a number of towns. Much of the booty was used to restore the treasures of the Temple.

Details of Asa's Reform (15:1–19)

We saw in 1 Chronicles how often the chronicler jumps back and forth along the time line. Thus, the events of chapter 15 may have occurred after Zerah's invasion, or they may be an additional glimpse of Asa's earlier reforms. The stimulus for the reforms described here came from the prophet Oded. He laid out for Asa two options—obedience to God followed by blessings or disobedience followed by rejection. "Don't let things get back to the turmoil of the time of the judges!" was Oded's message to Asa. The king complied with the prophet's injunction. He removed all forms of idolatry; even his grandmother Maacah was deposed, and her Asherah pole was publicly burned in the Kidron Valley.

Asa's Compromises (16:1–14)

Asa did not descend into idolatry as his two predecessors had done. Nevertheless, he did back away from his total devotion to God. We see events in this chapter that led from negligence in his trust in God to increased evil actions. By this time the king of Israel, the Northern Kingdom, was Baasha (already the founder of a second dynasty in the north). Baasha was no doubt irritated by the way in which many of his subjects were streaming into the kingdom of Judah. He may also have had his eyes on the newfound wealth of the Southern Kingdom. So Baasha made an alliance with Ben-Hadad, king of Aram, to invade Judah.

When Asa got wind of this threat, he took the treasures of the Temple and bribed King

The oath to kill all idol worshipers sounds harsh to modern ears, but this was precisely what had been commanded by God at Sinai (Exod. 22:20). The people of Israel were in a different position than gentile Christians are today. We are not called to be God's people in the physical and political sense in which the Israelites were called during Old Testament days. Our calling is different; we are not to use physical or political force to defend our beliefs. At the same time, it is good to remind ourselves that truth does matter and that not all beliefs and practices are acceptable in God's eyes.

Ben-Hadad with them to abandon his alliance with Baasha in order to join him. Ben-Hadad's word was for sale, and Asa's price was right. This meant that Baasha had to discontinue his plans, and he even lost some border towns in the process.

Asa's diplomacy did not please the Lord, however. It showed Asa's lack of trust in God. The prophet Hanani denounced Asa for placing confidence in a pagan ruler ahead of trust in the Lord, who had provided victory over Zerah. Never again would Asa's land enjoy peace. Rather than repent, Asa jailed the prophet and went on to suppress dissent among the people through forcible means. Asa and God were becoming increasingly estranged.

When Asa became ill, he did not turn to God for help but to the physicians (v. 12). Nonetheless, upon his death, Asa's body was perfumed thoroughly and buried with great honor.

We ought not to use this verse as an argument for believers to stay away from physicians and modern medicines. These kinds of doctors did not exist at that time; the "physicians" in Asa's day probably combined physical healing with pagan beliefs. The most advanced physicians of the day were Egyptian. Thus, Asa's guilt may have been twofold: turning away from God and turning toward questionable practitioners of healing.

■ *Asa was a good king through most of his*
■ *reign. He attempted to keep his kingdom free*
■ *of idol worship, and God granted him a*
■ *miraculous victory. But his alliance with a*
■ *pagan king brought a sad ending to his reign.*

JEHOSHAPHAT (17:1–20:37)

Jehoshaphat may have been coregent with his father Asa during the last two years of Asa's illness. When he came to the throne, he picked up where Asa should have left off. Jehoshaphat renewed the reforms of the land to remove all items of false worship and to restore the true worship of God. Once again, the king's program included the removal of all "high places." But with poignant repetitiveness, we read that Jehoshaphat was not able to accomplish this task thoroughly (20:33). The reason for this lack of success is that the people's hearts were not in the reforms. A superficial reform is not the same as a genuine commitment to God. In many ways, Jehoshaphat's life paralleled that of his father Asa. In spite of his initial commitments, he made some poor decisions. Nevertheless, on the whole, Jehoshaphat was the best king the Southern Kingdom had enjoyed since the division of the united kingdom.

Jehoshaphat's Reforms (17:1–9)

In addition to cleansing the land of idolatry, Jehoshaphat instituted another reform. He commissioned five of his officials, in the company of certain Levites and priests, to go about the kingdom teaching the Law. Perhaps Jehoshaphat had learned from his father's experience that commanding the people to obey God did not accomplish much if they were not given instruction in how to obey. The lesson plan for these itinerant teachers was the book of the Law—the five books of Moses, or the Pentateuch.

Jehoshaphat's Power (17:10–19)

With his usual love for lists, the author of Chronicles presents us with an inventory of the king's might. Jehoshaphat received much wealth in tribute; he was able to strengthen his cities; and he was able to raise an imposing army.

Jehoshaphat's Bad Alliance with Ahab (18:1–19:3)

There should have been little good for a man of God to see in the Northern Kingdom. Nevertheless, Jehoshaphat made an alliance with Ahab by having his son Jehoahaz marry the daughter of Ahab and Jezebel—Athaliah by name. This

Jehoshaphat was the fourth king of the Southern Kingdom. By this time, the Northern Kingdom had been through seven kings. Jeroboam's son, Nadab, had been killed by Baasha, whose son, Elah, in turn was killed by Zimri. Zimri's reign over Israel lasted only a week before he was assassinated, and Omri took over. Now Omri's son, Ahab, was on the throne. The Omri dynasty made several innovations; they located their capital in the city of Samaria and established the worship of Baal as the official religion of Israel.

compact would shortly prove disastrous for the Southern Kingdom. Having set up the alliance, Jehoshaphat consented to join Ahab in going to war against the Arameans (the same people with whom Baasha first, then Asa, had made an alliance). Jehoshaphat followed up his agreement with the suggestion that the two kings should also find out what God had to say about this matter. Keep in mind that Ahab was known as a dedicated worshiper of Baal, and his wife, Jezebel, had earlier declared genocide on all true worshipers of God.

Thus, in a procedure that could only be construed as pure mockery, Ahab paraded his prophetic lackeys to declare their false prophecies of a successful campaign. Jehoshaphat saw through the charade and urged Ahab to find yet another prophet. Ahab gave in reluctantly and had Micaiah brought forth, although he knew this prophet would not give a positive message.

True to form, after the kings did not want to accept Micaiah's initial flippant statement, the true prophet predicted disaster for Ahab. Micaiah's faithfulness to his calling earned him a slap and then life in prison. So Ahab and Jehoshaphat set out with their armies. Ahab thought he could escape God's verdict by disguising himself as a common soldier, but he was killed by a stray arrow. Jehoshaphat was able to return to Jerusalem, where he earned a firm rebuke from Jehu, a prophet, for having joined himself to the wicked Ahab.

The New Testament warns believers against being unequally yoked with unbelievers (2 Cor. 6:14–16). There is spiritual as well as practical wisdom to this injunction. It is impossible for regenerate and unregenerate people to exist together as though there were no difference.

Jehoshaphat's Judicial Reforms (19:4–11)

After the misadventure with Ahab, Jehoshaphat returned to his internal obligations. He traveled throughout his land from border to border to exhort the people to belief and obedience. He installed a judicial system with judges who had specific jurisdictions, compelling them to be scrupulous in their duties. In Jerusalem the king appointed a Levitical court, presided over by the high priest; this organization may have been ancestor to the Sanhedrin, the Jewish council at the time of Jesus.

Jehoshaphat's War with the Ammonites and Moabites (20:1–29)

When new trouble brewed, Jehoshaphat passed the test that Asa had failed in later life. He learned to trust God and was able to enjoy a miraculous victory.

By the time Jehoshaphat got word of the invasion, the army was already on the west bank of the Dead Sea in Judaean territory. Jehoshaphat was distraught, but he knew that his help would have to come from the Lord. He declared a fast and led the people in a public prayer which entreated the Lord to come to the rescue of His people. He reminded God that He had promised to save Israel in just this kind of situation when He responded to Solomon's prayer (7:13–14).

The answer from God came to Jehoshaphat by way of a prophet from the tribe of Levi named Jahaziel, a descendant of Asaph, David's minister of music. Jahaziel's prophecy was Psalm 83, a reassurance that God would give the victory. The prophet told the king where to go on the next day, but he indicated that he would not have to fight. Some Levites led in praise of God.

The next day Jehoshaphat and his army set out in unmilitary fashion, singing and praising the Lord. And when they came to the supposed place of engagement, they found nothing but corpses. The soldiers had turned on one another

Given the situation in the Fertile Crescent, it was only a matter of time before the eastern and southeastern neighbors of Judah—Ammon, Edom, and Moab—would assert themselves militarily. During the time of David and Solomon, when Egypt was weak and there was no strong power in Mesopotamia, these nations had been subjugated by the United Kingdom. Now Egypt was a power again, the Assyrians were stirring in northern Mesopotamia, Aram was causing trouble, and the kingdom was divided. One wonders why it took so long for the Transjordanian nations to pick a fight with Judah.

"Beracah" means the Valley of Praise.

and annihilated themselves. All that was left for Jehoshaphat to do was to lead his people in further praise. The location where this took place was known from this day on as "Beracah."

Close-out on Jehoshaphat—and a Final Bad mark (20:31–37)

The chronicler now proceeds to his usual formula for summarizing a king's life. Jehoshaphat comes away with good marks. However, the chronicler does not leave the matter there. He indicates that Jehoshaphat did not learn a lesson from his ill-timed adventure with Ahab. Instead he renewed the alliance with Ahab's son and successor, Ahaziah. This time the two kings decided to go into the shipbuilding business. Again Jehoshaphat received a prophet's rebuke, and as punishment all the ships were destroyed. But this was only the beginning of the trouble caused by the alliance.

- Jehoshaphat of Judah was a godly man. Yet
- he allied himself with the ungodly rulers of
- the Northern Kingdom.

JEHORAM (21:1–20)

As soon as Jehoshaphat died, the results of the marriage alliance with the house of Ahab became obvious. Jehoram, the new occupant of the throne, displayed the same wickedness as his father-in-law, Ahab, urged on by his wife, Athaliah, the daughter of Jezebel (v. 6). He killed all of his siblings, lest one of them should usurp his throne, and he propagated idolatrous religion. But divine judgment was spontaneous: Virtually everything that could go wrong for Jehoram did.

The nations surrounding his kingdom began to break away from Jewish overlordship. All but one of his sons were taken from him. Elijah, who had been preaching against the abuses of the Northern Kingdom, sent a letter to Jehoram, predicting a horrible death for the king as punishment for his sins. This event did come about, and Jehoram died of a very painful disease. No one was sorry to see him gone. The chronicler tells us that the only reason why God did not abolish the whole kingdom at that moment was because of His promise to David (v. 7).

- *Jehoram was as evil as his in-laws in the*
- *Northern Kingdom. God sent immediate*
- *retribution for his apostasy.*

AHAZIAH (22:1–12)

 To understand the events of this chapter, it is helpful to have a clear grasp of the family relationships involved.

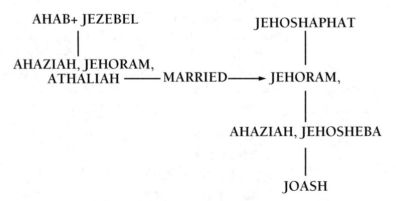

Ahaziah, son of Jehoram and Athaliah, continued the corrupt practices of his father, as modeled by his relatives of the Northern Kingdom and encouraged by his mother. We can speculate

75

how close the kingdom of Judah came to being subsumed under the kingship of the north, but God would not let this happen. The Lord appointed Jehu the next king of the north to destroy the family of Ahab. Providentially, Ahaziah was in the Northern Kingdom at the time calling on the northern king, and Ahaziah was included in the purge. Since he was a young man, there was no immediate claimant to the throne. His son Joash was still an infant. So Athaliah, his mother, claimed the throne for herself and executed every member of the family of David—except Joash, who was concealed by Ahaziah's sister Jehosheba.

- *Ahaziah was as evil as Jehoram; he was*
- *killed in the retribution which God sent to*
- *the house of Ahab by the hand of Jehu.*

JOASH (23:1–24:27)

The rule of the land by Athaliah was unauthorized, so she was not an official queen. In her six years on the throne, she did her best to transform Judah into a throroughly ungodly nation. Providentially again, her relatives to the north had been eliminated, so she did not have the forces of the kingdom of Israel to back her up.

Joash's Enthronement and Early Rule (23:1–24:14)

Jehoiada, the high priest, had been keeping Joash under his protection in concealment. When the youngster was seven years old, Jehoiada displayed him publicly as the king in the Temple and ordered Athaliah's execution; apparently the self-proclaimed queen died unsupported and unmourned. Now followed the good years of Joash's reign.

As long as Jehoiada was available to guide him, Joash proved himself a devoted and adept king. An important project that Jehoiada directed Joash to undertake was the renovation of the Temple, which had been neglected and even vandalized during the last few reigns. When the project lagged because of insufficient funding, the young king and his advisor implemented the Temple tax first decreed by Moses (Exod. 30:14) and used that money for both workmen and materials.

The Temple tax was still in effect at the time of Jesus. When Peter did not think that they could pay it, Jesus miraculously produced the necessary coin from the mouth of a fish (Matt. 17:27).

Joash's Later Rule (24:15–27)

As good as Joash was early in his reign, the chronicler shows that he was faithful only as long as he had Jehoiada by his side to direct him. The priest-advisor died at the age of 130 and was buried among the kings of Judah. Immediately Joash reverted to the form of his predecessors, reinstituting various forms of Canaanite idol worship and leading his people back into apostasy. The Lord sent several prophets, and then He confronted Joash in the person of Zechariah, the son of Jehoiada. Joash's perversity was so entrenched by now that he executed the son of the man who had preserved his life and made him king.

What a poignant lesson Joash provides on the need for maturity! Parents and older Christians need to provide guidance to children and new believers. But guidance is not the same thing as dependency; the goal of Christian instruction is for believers to become so knowledgeable in God's Word that they function properly even if they do not have immediate access to someone who will direct them. Eventually, Christians should become teachers themselves (1 John 2:27; Heb. 5:12; 2 Tim. 2:2).

Joash suffered severe punishments for his faithlessness. Aram invaded and looted Jerusalem, and Joash himself was severely wounded in the conflict. Two of his own subjects finished the job. Joash, the boy king who had carried the hopes of the faithful among his people, died in disgrace and did not receive a full royal burial.

- *Joash was faithful to God as long as he was*
- *under the tutelage of Jehoiada, the priest.*
- *When the priest died, Joash immediately fell*
- *into idolatry.*

AMAZIAH (25:1–28)

Amaziah's reign was characterized by mediocrity. The chronicler's judgment is that he followed the Lord, but not wholeheartedly. Compared to the second half of his father Joash's reign, he did put the kingdom on a better footing, but he wound up compromising himself right into disaster. Amaziah had the killers of Joash executed, and he did not extend this judgment to his sons, in keeping with Deuteronomy 24:16. But Amaziah's compromising nature came out in connection with his first military venture. He recruited an army with warriors from his own area as well as from the Northern Kingdom. When a prophet convicted him that he should not use troops from the apostate Northern Kingdom to fight God's war, the king's immediate response was to worry about the lost funds if those mercenaries would not fight for him.

Nevertheless, he set out for the area of the Dead Sea and won a thorough victory against Seir, the Edomites. His return from the victory was marred by two problems: First, he brought back Edomite deities and worshiped them. Second, he learned that the Israelite troops he had sent back had caused havoc in his land. Amaziah's idolatry earned him the rebuke of a prophet, but this time the king ignored the warning. Then he insisted on going to war against the Northern Kingdom. The end result was the disaster foretold by the prophet. Amaziah was captured, and Jerusalem was plundered.

In cryptic terms, the account in Chronicles alludes to the following sequence of events: Amaziah lived as hostage in Samaria for ten years; upon Jehoahash's death, he was released and lived for another fifteen years. During this time, his son, Uzziah, was installed as coregent in Jerusalem. Amaziah's assassination concluded a period in which he had long ceased to be in power.

■ *Amaziah was a mediocre king who suffered*
■ *the consequences of his compromises.*

UZZIAH (26:1–23)

Uzziah had a long reign (fifty-two years), but much of that time was overlapped on both ends by coregency. This king's reign was character-ized by his devotion to God and consequent suc-cess. His accomplishments led to spiritual pride. Uzziah sought to emulate the pagan practice of combining the offices of king and priest in spite of the Levitical priests' protests. He was struck with leprosy and had to finish his reign in seclu-sion. The day-to-day affairs of the government went to his son Jotham for the rest of his life.

Historically, this time period, which also dovetailed with the long and prosperous reign of Jeroboam 2 in Israel, was a time of relative security. Egypt had become quiet again, and Assyria was not yet rattling its sabres too closely to Jerusalem. Thus, Uzziah was able to regain some of the territory lost by the previous kings and to reestablish a presence on the Red Sea by rebuilding Eloth.

■ *Uzziah's reign was a time of peace and*
■ *prosperity, but this king brought trouble*
■ *upon himself with his deliberate violation of*
■ *God's rules.*

JOTHAM (27:1–8)

Jotham receives nothing but plaudits from the chronicler. He served the Lord, and the Lord blessed him with success. At this time the Assyrians were beginning their conquests, but Jotham was able to fortify his position by reconquering the land of the Ammonites. And so the kingdom still enjoyed security and prosperity. Still, appearances can be superficial, and they were in this case. The telling phrase occurs in verse 2b. In spite of Jotham's personal piety, the people of the land continued their pagan practices.

- Jotham attempted to restore the land to faithfulness in its worship of God. He carried out a thorough but ineffective reform.

AHAZ (28:1–27)

Baal was the highest god of Canaanite religion. Baal was worshiped on altars, usually in the vicinity of Asherah sites, and his devotees also committed sexual perversions. In addition, the worship of Baal included the sacrifice of human firstborn sons, apparently in order to arouse Baal to promote the fertility of fields so there would be a plentiful harvest.

If a bad decision was a possibility, you could count on King Ahaz to make it. Ahaz took religious corruption to a new low in the Southern Kingdom. He was a devout worshiper of Baal to the point where he sacrificed his own son to this cruel god. He also closed the doors of the Temple so true worship of the Lord could not continue. As a result—and for the chronicler apostasy always brought affliction—Ahaz suffered defeat from surrounding nations. The Arameans and Israelites from the north routed his troops. Then the Edomites and even the Philistines exacted their quota of punishment.

In order to regain some semblance of security, Ahaz made a deal that backfired on him. He entered an alliance with Assyria, which was creating havoc in the Northern Kingdom. Assyria was more than willing to take all the treasures out of the Temple which Ahaz offered in payment. The king even worshiped the Assyrian gods—and received nothing in return. Of all the nations that conquered Israel from time to time, the Assyrians were the most barbaric and least trustworthy.

Obed's Plea For Israel's Judaean Prisoners (vv. 9–16)

While Ahaz was moving from failure to failure, a prophet named Oded carried out a mission on behalf of a number of captured soldiers. He went to Samaria and pointed out to the leaders of Israel that, even though they were used by God to bring punishment on Judah, they were not free to go beyond their immediate victory. After all, Oded said, they already had enough to answer for apart from mistreating their Judahite brothers. The Israelites complied. This good deed did not stave off the imminent punishment for the Northern Kingdom. In 733 B.C. the Assyrian king Tiglath Pileser III carried into captivity the tribes on the east side of the Jordan and in the northern parts of Israel (2 Kings 15:29). Then in 722 B.C. Shalmaneser V and his successor Sargon II conquered Samaria and the rest of the kingdom (2 Kings 17:6).

Ahaz's misguided military alliances became the occasion for one of the best-loved verses of the Old Testament. Isaiah, the prophet, exhorted Ahaz to trust in the Lord rather than fearing his neighbors and offered a sign in validation of God's faithfulness. When Ahaz refused, Isaiah proclaimed, "The Lord himself will give you a sign: The virgin will be with child and will give birth to a son, and will call him Immanuel" (Isa. 7:14).

- ■ *Ahaz was an evil king who compounded idol-*
- ■ *atry with bad political judgment.*

HEZEKIAH (29:1–32:33)

Hezekiah has been called the second Solomon, and in many ways this designation fits this wise and righteous king. With Hezekiah we have the high point of the Southern Kingdom. No ruler since David and Solomon had attained such greatness. Sadly, none after Hezekiah would either. He restored the Temple and the proper worship services; he led the people in a grand revival; and he experienced the wondrous protection of God when Jerusalem was attacked by the Assyrians. Second Chronicles gives four chapters to Hezekiah and his reign. Fittingly for the chronicler, three of those chapters are devoted to Hezekiah's religious reforms, and only one to the attempted conquest by Sennacherib, king of the Assyrians.

Hezekiah's Reclaiming of the Temple (29:1–36)

Ahaz, Hezekiah's father, had barred the doors of the Temple and shut down worship of the Lord. When Hezekiah came to power, he began a revival of Temple worship. He called the priests and Levites together. First there was a trickle—then a steady stream—of Temple workers returning to Jerusalem to resume their appointed tasks. In order to be usable, the Temple had to be made ritually clean, which required that the priests and Levites purify themselves first.

Purification was an important part of the Old Testament law. There were several ways in which one could ritually contaminate oneself, such as contact with a corpse or a bodily fluid (blood, semen, or menses). Further, touching anyone who was in a state of impurity would pass the contamination on. Anyone who had become impure had to go through a cleansing procedure. This ritual could last from one evening (for bodily discharges) to 36 days (for childbirth). Until a person was cleansed, he or she could not enter the Temple area.

When the Temple was purified, Hezekiah held a dedication ceremony which consisted of burnt offerings. The chronicler points out a few interesting sidelights: the names of the Levites who took the lead in the preparations (vv. 12–14), Hezekiah restored the Temple music as well as the sacrifices (vv. 25–26, 30), some of the Levites were more diligent than the priests in their purifications (v. 34*b*), and this event created joy among the people (v. 36). What joy returning to the Lord can bring!

Hezekiah's Big Passover (30:1–27)

In order to carry on the revival and extend it to all the people, Hezekiah called a nationwide Passover celebration. Heralds traveled through Judah and even to Israel to invite people to come to Jerusalem for this feast. Hezekiah's invitation was motivated by the idea that perhaps a true revival might turn back the troubles which the country was suffering.

Many devout people, including some from the north, accepted the invitation. Given the time necessary for people to travel and to undergo the required purifications, it was impossible to hold this observance in the required month. So the leaders invoked the provision of Numbers 9:9–11, which allowed them to hold Passover a month later. As the seven days of Passover progressed, more people continued to show up, and more priests and Levites took up their duties.

When it was discovered that a large number of people from the Northern Kingdom were partaking of the lamb and unleavened bread without having undertaken the necessary ritual cleansing, Hezekiah himself interceded with God on their behalf. God honored this request because these people were seeking God in the right attitude. As the ranks of participants and purified Levites continued to swell, a second week of Passover was added so all who desired could join the celebration.

Hezekiah's Continued Reform (31:1–21)

Hezekiah was not content to reinstitute worship of the true God or to abolish idolatry. Like his ancestor David almost three hundred years earlier, the king made provisions that the service in the Temple might continue. He revived the

Passover was instituted by God through Moses (Exod. 12:1–28). It was for all practical purposes the same as the Feast of Unleavened Bread. The Passover included three compulsory parts: eating a lamb, eating unleavened bread, and retelling the story of the escape from Egypt. This festival was a tangible representation of what it meant to be God's redeemed people.

divisions and shifts for Temple workers that David had instituted and resumed the collection which went to provide for their welfare.

Hezekiah's Success and Preservation (32:1–33)

The chronicler's account of Hezekiah's reign concludes with the dramatic events of this king's life. Most outstanding among these was the failed attempt by Sennacherib of Assyria to conquer Jerusalem. Condensing several campaigns into one picture, the chronicler emphasizes Hezekiah's faith and God's miraculous preservation of His city. The Assyrian king sought to taunt the Jews by claiming that their God could not stand up to him. But God sent His angel, and in one night He annihilated the entire Assyrian army; the Assyrian king had to return home in humiliation. This victory, which God brought about for Hezekiah, earned the king great honor in the eyes of his people. With the Assyrians out of the picture, he enjoyed peace and prosperity (vv. 27–29).

Hezekiah's accomplishments rival those of Solomon on a smaller scale; his building projects included a water tunnel in case of any future invasions. Hezekiah had much to be proud about, but his pride was also his greatest flaw. After a miraculous cure of an otherwise fatal disease, the king became so arrogant that he earned a reproof from God (vv. 25–26). And pride was also a vice he could not forego in bragging before a group of Babylonian envoys (v. 31).

Nevertheless, Hezekiah was probably the best king the Southern Kingdom had. He was buried with great honor, and the future of the land was left in the hands of his young son, Manasseh.

Sennacherib was king of Assyria from 705 B.C. until 681 B.C. He is well known to us, not only from the biblical accounts, but also from his own records, known as the Taylor Cylinder, found in A.D. 1830. His writings show him as a cruel conqueror who subdued Babylon and even defeated the Egyptian army. In describing his campaign against Judah, Sennacherib boasted that he shut up Hezekiah in Jerusalem like a bird in a cage, but he did not mention that he had to withdraw in defeat before he had finished this campaign.

■ *Hezekiah was a great king in all respects:*
■ *spiritually, politically, and materially. He*
■ *restored proper worship and was able to*
■ *enjoy a miraculous rescue from the Assyrian*
■ *onslaught.*

MANASSEH (33:1–20)

The account of Manasseh's reign in 2 Chronicles consists of two parts: his sin with its dire repercussions and his repentance with its short-term consequences.

Manasseh's Sin (vv. 1–9)

Manasseh outdid his pagan neighbors with his wickedness. In addition to the worship of Canaanite deities, including sacrificing his sons to Baal, he cultivated Babylonian customs as well. The only form of religion excluded was the worship of the one true God. The Temple of God became nothing more to him than a place to erect pagan idols.

Manasseh's Punishment and Repentance (vv. 10–20)

For a long time Manasseh ignored the warnings from God; but, then, the inevitable punishment occurred. Ashurbanipal of Assyria subjugated Jerusalem and deported Manasseh, leading him with hooks all the way to Babylon. There Manasseh came to repentance. God allowed him to return to Jerusalem, where he instituted a restoration of the Temple and a revival of the worship of God. The people complied outwardly but inwardly they maintained the same pagan practices; they just did them in the name of the Lord (v. 17). Manasseh died a short time

During Manasseh's reign, Palestine continued in the shadow of Assyrian might. The Assyrian king Ashurbanipal, who was not usually as destructive as his predecessors, undertook a successful conquest against Jerusalem. At the same time, Baylonian culture also started to become influential. We find Manasseh resorting to Babylonian practices, such as astrology and seances.

later, having spent most of his long reign corrupting the country.

- *In spite of Manasseh's eventual repentance*
- *and attempts at reform, the heritage he*
- *bestowed was his wickedness and idolatry.*

AMON (33:21–25)

Amon's short reign does not contribute much to the story other than to show how ineffective Manasseh's reform had been. As soon as this young king came to the throne, the land reverted to the paganism of his father's reign. Amon was assassinated only two years into his reign. The assassins were executed, and his son Josiah, the next person in line from the family of David, was crowned king of Judah.

- *The best thing about Amon's reign was its*
- *brevity. He also bequeathed a legacy of evil.*

JOSIAH (34:1–35:27)

Josiah was the Southern Kingdom's second boy king (the other being Joash). This eight-year-old came to the throne in a time of turmoil. Yet as he matured, he gradually instituted reforms which eventually culminated in another national Passover in which the people dedicated themselves to the Lord. At the heart of the reform was the rediscovery of the Book of the Law.

Josiah's Early Reforms (34:1–6)

When Josiah was sixteen years old, he was converted to the faith of the true God. This event must have occurred apart from any direct

Manasseh's repentance (which, incidentally is not recorded in 2 Kings) demonstrates that there is no limit to the grace of God. Jesus said, "It is not the healthy who need a doctor, but the sick" (Matt. 9:12), and the apostle Paul wrote, "I was shown mercy so that in me, the worst of sinners, Christ Jesus might display his unlimited patience as an example for those who would believe on him and receive eternal life" (1 Tim. 1:16). Let us not fall into the same trap as the older brother in the parable of the prodigal son (Luke 15:11–32) and judge who is worthy of the grace of God. It is intended for the unworthy.

knowledge of Scripture (since it would not be rediscovered until later), and no people who might have influenced the young king are named. Josiah's understanding was clear enough to realize that faith in God and idolatry were incompatible. Thus, he instituted a purge of paganism throughout the land. Josiah was able to extend his reform into the area which had once been the Northern Kingdom and which was now inhabited by a remnant of Israelites.

Rediscovery of the Book of the Law (34:8–18)

Only after the initial removal of idols from the land did Josiah's reform extend to the Temple. The king was now twenty-six years old; it had been seventy-five years since Hezekiah's reign. Except for the duration of Manasseh's brief revival, the Temple had been abused. It obviously needed physical restoration as well as spiritual rededication. So Josiah sent the Levites to collect the Temple tax throughout the land and to use this money for the renovations.

The chronicler pays special attention to the fact that the Temple musicians had supervisory duties. But it was the high priest Hilkiah who made the startling discovery of the Book of the Law. Given the concerted efforts of Manasseh and Amon to suppress God's revelation, it is no wonder that the book became lost. But suddenly, here was revelation from God Himself!

Reading the Book and Repentance (34:19–33)

What a shock it must have been for Josiah and the other leaders to come upon this neglected book! Undoubtedly there was joy, but we read mostly of dread—the realization that God's law had been spurned. In response to Josiah's acts of repentance on behalf of the whole nation, the

The "Book of the Law" could have been the first five books of Moses (Genesis through Deuteronomy) or Deuteronomy alone or some combination thereof. Since curses are specifically mentioned (v. 24), and since they play such a prominent part in Deuteronomy, this book must at least have been included in this scroll.

The balance of power in the Fertile Crescent was shifting in Josiah's day. By now Assyria had lost its power, partially due to an invasion of Scythian tribesmen. Nineveh was destroyed in 612 B.C. while Josiah was on the throne in Judah. Babylon was not yet mighty, and Egypt was struggling to find its place in the world again. All of this would change drastically just a few years after Josiah became king.

The so-called "ten lost tribes" of the Northern Kingdom were not completely lost. Recall that in 1 Chronicles 9:3, people from Ephraim and Manasseh were included among those who returned from Exile.

Under King Nabopolassar, the ancient kingdom of Babylon reestablished itself and gave signs of becoming the dominant power in the Fertile Crescent. Neco, the pharaoh of Egypt, attempted to stop Babylonia and achieve supremacy in the Fertile Crescent. He gathered a large army and marched up to the ancient Hittite city of Carchemish, where he attempted to squelch Babylonian ambitions in a huge battle. The decisive battle took place in 605 B.C. Neco was thoroughly defeated, and Babylonia became the supreme power.

prophetess Huldah spoke encouraging words from God. Even though there would be a retribution for Israel's sins, Josiah would be spared that event, and he would be buried in peace (though his violent death was due to his own foolishness). Josiah realized that his responsibility entailed making the book available to the people, so he held a public reading of the Law, renewed the covenant with God, and gave himself to the removal of idolatry with fresh vigor.

Josiah's Great Passover (35:1–19)

Reminiscent of David's installation of the ark, Solomon's dedication of the Temple, or Hezekiah's Passover, Josiah also held a huge festival—once again a Passover. In fact, his celebration outdid Hezekiah's in magnitude. One last time in the era prior to the Exile, the priests assumed their proper duties along with the Levites, the gatekeepers, and the musicians.

Josiah's Death (35:20–27)

But even this godly king disobeyed God and wound up having to suffer the consequences. Toward the end of Josiah's reign, world events took a drastic turn.

Josiah had enjoyed relative peace and independence throughout his reign. Now that the Egyptian army of Pharaoh Neco was marching north through Israel on its way to Carchemish, Josiah feared for his sovereignty and attempted to stop Neco and his troops. Perhaps Josiah felt that God wanted him to do this; even assurances from Neco that it was not God's will for Josiah to hinder him did not dissuade the Jewish king. The battle between Egypt and Judah took place in the plain of Megiddo. This shows that Neco had already marched up the coast past Josiah's territory without attacking Jerusalem. Josiah's death was completely unnecessary. Josiah was buried and mourned as both a great king and a spiritual hero.

- *Josiah's reign is poignant because of his sin-*
- *cere and thorough reform—the last one*
- *before the Exile—and because of his prema-*
- *ture death.*

JEHOAHAZ (36:1–3)

The last four kings of Judah were neither strong nor godly. They ignored God and attempted to escape their certain doom by concocting treasonous alliances. Jehoahaz succeeded his father, Josiah, after the battle at Megiddo. When Neco returned three months later, he deposed Jehoahaz, carried him into Exile in Egypt, and exacted a sizeable tribute from Judah.

Megiddo was a city and fortress located strategically in the transition area from the Mediterranean coast to the inland plain. It had been fortified by Solomon and refortified by Ahab. It even had an underground well to supply water during times of an enemy siege. The "mountain of Megiddo" is "Har Meggido" from which we get the term *Armageddon*. The final battle of human history will take place on this plain where Neco defeated Josiah.

- *Jehoahaz reigned only three months before*
- *he was dethroned by the pharaoh of Egypt.*

JEHOIAKIM (36:4–7)

Pharaoh Neco installed a king of his own over Judah—Jehoahaz's older brother, Eliakim. Furthermore, the Egytian king changed Eliakim's name to Jehoiakim. Both names mean the same thing—"God raises up!"—but the second version includes God's covenant name *Yahweh*. For some reason this suited the pharaoh's purposes better. Despite his pious name, Jehoiakim was no man of God (2 Kings 23:35–37). During Jehoiakim's reign, Nebuchadnezzar came to Jerusalem. The Babylonian king removed treasures from the Temple

Three different times Nebuchadnezzar deported Jews from Jerusalem. The first one occurred under Jehoiakim. The Babylonians carried off treasure and a few young men. This first deportation included Daniel and his three friends (Dan. 1:1–4).

The second deportation occurred under Jehoiachin. This time Nebuchadnezzar expatriated thousands of Jews and relocated them to Babylon. These people were designated for slave labor on a canal excavation project. Among them was Ezekiel (Ezek. 1:1). Thus, a sizable number of Jews was already in Babylon by the time Jerusalem finally fell.

and carried a group of young nobles, including the king, to Babylon.

■ *Jehoiakim's rule culminated in the first*
■ *deportation to Babylon.*

JEHOIACHIN (36:8–9)

We learn very little of Jehoiachin's reign from Chronicles. He was the teenage son of Jehoiakim, and his policies were no better than those of his father. But he reigned only about three months before he was taken into Exile in Babylon. This time Nebuchadnezzar also carried away a large group of people as slave labor.

■ *Jehoiachin continued the legacy of unfaith-*
■ *fulness and incompetence. Three months into*
■ *his reign, Nechuchadnezzar deported other*
■ *Jewish citizens to Babylon.*

ZEDEKIAH (36:10–13)

Nebuchadnezzar installed Zedekiah, brother of Jehoahaz and Jehoiakim and uncle of Jehoiachin, as the final king. Zedekiah was compelled to swear loyalty to the Babylonian king and to pay a tribute. He cared for divine truth as little as did his predecessors, but he had delusions that God would deliver him from Babylonia. He made an alliance with Egypt against his Babylonian overlords. When Nebuchadnezzar found out about Zedekiah's treason, he sent his troops to Jerusalem, destroyed the Temple, and carried virtually the entire population to Exile in Babylon.

■ *Zedekiah presided over the final demise of*
■ *Jerusalem and the third deportation. He con-*
■ *tributed to this scenario through his pride*
■ *and arrogance.*

THE EXILE (36:14–21)

The defeat at the hands of the Babylonians was no accident, according to the chronicler; it was the direct result of Judah's disobedience. The list of sins committed include: idolatry, violation of the sanctity of the Temple, and rejection of the prophets. As a result, God sent the Babylonians (v. 17) to bring punishment. The whole land was laid waste because the people were carried off. The chronicler comments that the devastation of the land fulfilled Jeremiah's prophecy: The people had not observed the sabbaths of the land (Lev. 25:1–2; 26:34), so now God was enforcing His ordinance (see Jer. 25:9–12).

The third deportation involved the destruction of Jerusalem and most of the people of Judah. Only the aged and infirm were allowed to remain. Jeremiah the prophet ministered in Jerusalem in the years leading up to its destruction (Jer. 39). Assyrian policy had been to substitute new people for those taken into Exile; the Babylonians did not bother.

■ *The Exile was punishment for the people's*
■ *violation of God's ordinances.*

RETURN FROM THE EXILE (36:22–23)

Second Chronicles ends on a positive note. When Cyrus of Persia overthrew the Babylonians, he instituted an empire-wide policy of tolerance. God used a pagan king to redeem His people—just as Isaiah had prophesied in the days of Hezekiah. These verses are identical with Ezra 1:1–3*a*.

Cyrus first gave the Persian half of the Medo-Persian kingdom supremacy. Then he conquered Babylon and ruled his new empire from 539 to 530 B.C. Cyrus worshiped the Babylonian god Marduk, but he encouraged other people to be true to their own religions. The Jews were not the only exiled people who were allowed to return, and Cyrus encouraged other nations to build temples for their gods. In the time of Hezekiah, Isaiah confirmed that there would be a time of exile, and he predicted Cyrus' part in the return of God's people. Josephus tells us that Cyrus was first motivated to release the Jews when he read Isaiah's scroll and found his own name in the prophecy.

■ *In his grace, God restored His people to the*
■ *land by Cyrus' decree.*

QUESTIONS TO GUIDE YOUR STUDY

1. What were the strengths and weaknesses of each king of Judah?
2. What role did the Temple and its personnel (priests and Levites) play in the history of the Southern Kingdom?
3. What role did the word of God (prophets and Scripture) play in the history of the Southern Kingdom?

REFERENCE SOURCES

Archer, Gleason L. *A Survey of Old Testament Introduction*. Chicago: Moody Press, 1964.

Braun, Roddy. *1 Chronicles. Word Biblical Commentary*. Waco, Tex: Word Books, 1986.

Coggins, R. J. *The First and Second Books of the Chronicles*. New York: Cambridge University Press, 1976.

Dillard, Raymond D. *2 Chronicles. Word Biblical Commentary*. Waco, Tex: Word Books, 1987.

Myers, Jacob M. *I Chronicles. II Chronicles. The Anchor Bible*. Garden City, N.Y.: Doubleday, 1965.

Orr, James, ed. *The International Standard Bible Encyclopedia*. 4 vols. Grand Rapids, Mich.: Wm. B. Eerdmans, 1956.

Payne, J. Barton. "I and II Chronicles." *The Wycliffe Bible Commentary*. Charles F. Pfeiffer and Everett F. Harrion, eds.

Chicago: Moody Press, 1962, pp. 367–421.

Pfeiffer, Robert H. *Introduction to the Old Testament*. New York: Harper & Brothers, 1948.

Purkiser, W. T. *Exploring the Old Testament*. Kansas City: Beacon Hill Press, 1955.

Selman, Martin J. *1 Chronicles. 2 Chronicles*. Downers Grove, Ill.: InterVarsity Press, 1994.

Unger, Merrill F., ed. *Unger's Bible Dictionary*. Chicago: Moody Press, 1966.

Wilcock, Michael. "1 and 2 Chronicles." *New Bible Commentary: 21st Century Edition*. D. A. Carson, R. T. France, J. A. Motyer, and G. J. Wenham, eds. Downers Grove, Ill.: InterVarsity Press, 1994, pp. 388–419.

Wilson, Charles R. "First Chronicles," "Second Chronicles." *Wesleyan Bible Commentary*. Charles Carter, ed. Vol. 2, pp. 341–427.

Young, Edward J. *An Introduction to the Old Testament*. Grand Rapids: Wm. B. Eerdmans, 1953. *The Anchor Bible*. Garden City, N.Y.: Doubleday, 1965.

SHEPHERD'S NOTES

SHEPHERD'S NOTES

SHEPHERD'S
NOTES

SHEPHERD'S NOTES

SHEPHERD'S NOTES

SHEPHERD'S NOTES